The Indian Conservative

Praise for the Book

'In *The Indian Conservative* Jaithirth Rao makes an engaging case for why conservatism – in which he includes moderate Hindu Nationalism – is necessary for India. This is not a book that strives for balance. Rao is opinionated, with favourites in the pantheon of Indian leaders and intellectuals, as well as pet hates. It is, however, an important and erudite contribution to the debate as we ponder the future of India.'

Raghuram Rajan

'Ever since the British came, thinking Indians have been questioning how to modernize our tradition. Indians are conservative by nature, but can we tap into our rich roots to create a modern, conservative political identity? And can we achieve this without dividing ourselves or adopting majoritarian positions? Are there 'mystic chords of memory' that bind us and make us a nation? Read this absorbing book for answers. Even if you disagree, it will make you think.'

Gurcharan Das

'Classical Indian Conservatism has been a political and intellectual orphan for nearly five decades now. It has been defined purely in religious terms, following the lazy new definitions of the Left and the Right. Jaithirth Rao's book fills that very important gap and rekindles a debate dormant for too long. His is among the very few minds today that still combine modern rationalism with ideological conservatism and free economic thought. He is making a civil argument that the Right need not be synonymous with evil.'

Shekhar Gupta

The Indian
Conservative
A History of
Indian Right-Wing Thought

Jaithirth Rao

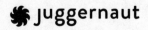

JUGGERNAUT BOOKS
KS House, 118 Shahpur Jat, New Delhi 110049, India

First published by Juggernaut Books 2019

10 9 8 7 6 5 4 3 2

P-ISBN: 978-93-5345-062-5
E-ISBN: 978-93-5345-063-2

Typeset in Adobe Caslon Pro by R. Ajith Kumar, Noida

Printed and bound at Thomson Press India Ltd

The Conservative is put on this earth in order to 'conserve'
the best part of his or her inheritance. In that spirit,
I dedicate this book to my grandfather Coimbatore
R. Raghavendra Rao, who was a lifelong scholar and
aficionado of the divine Tirukkural, which has to be one of
our finer legacies, worth preserving and learning from

Contents

Author's Note

There is an ancient tradition of right-wing thought in India, which I call conservatism. The BJP and the RSS, popularly seen as synonymous with the right-wing point of view, are offshoots of this school of thought, and though there are many similarities, there are many divergences too. I have used the word conservatism throughout the book so as not to confuse the reader.

Introduction

The objective of this book is to explore and position the philosophical underpinnings of modern Indian conservatism, as well as to present contemporary courses of action in five distinct spheres: the economic, the cultural, the social, the political and the aesthetic. While no such attempt can possibly cover everything comprehensively, here is an attempt at a wide-ranging examination. Indian conservatism has received scant attention from academia and rarely gets media attention except in its most caricatured form. Its relationship to indigenous intellectual sources going back to antiquity and to Western traditions that are derived from the work of the eighteenth-century English philosopher and public figure Edmund Burke have rarely been seen as worth analysing or understanding, let alone celebrating.

Intellectual discourse in India, especially from the second half of the twentieth century and into the current century, has been dominated by paradigms borrowed from the metropolitan centres of the West – the grammars used have been Marxist, Freudian, postmodern and so on, with India contributing a subaltern historical school within the postmodern dialogues. This has also been the case with intellectual discourse about India in Western academic and journalistic circles.

A certain amount of political discourse, not fully acknowledged as intellectual by academia, has had a particular Hindu nationalist flavour associated with it. This point of view has so far remained on the peripheries of academic respectability, within the entrenched cloisters of universities in India and in the West. Any attempt at seriously studying conservatism, let alone contributing to an ongoing intellectual conversation with it, has been avoided simply by using the assumption that at least in the political sphere, Indian conservatism is nothing but a Siamese twin attached to what is externally described as Hindu nationalism.

This attempt at defining conservatism by its intellectual adversaries ensconced in powerful academic positions – and in so attempting, also limiting its appeal – has, I believe, not been constructive for the broader development of healthy, mutually respectful points of view. Students and the general public end up as losers if the various brilliant strands and schools of conservative thought are excluded from study and contemplation.

I would reject the position that Hindu nationalism is not a respectable political doctrine worth studying. However, the fundamental argument that keeps recurring is whether Hindu nationalism is a subset within the broad tent of Indian conservatism or whether Indian conservatism and Hindu nationalism have some elements that overlap and others that do not. The creative tension around this argument is particularly highlighted when we confront extreme and violent elements in the Hindu nationalist fold. While moderate Hindu nationalism, which emphasizes Indian cultural unities, can be seen as a legitimate movement within a broader conservative umbrella, Hindu extremism remains more problematic.

~

Conservatism is a school of philosophy which is not characterized by rigid contours or definitions. It believes that human beings as individuals and as communities have evolved over time, developing laws, institutions, cultures, norms and associations. This evolutionary process undoubtedly contributes to practical utility. The process itself is one of trial and error. It is grounded in a deep sense of empiricism, focused heavily on what works on the ground and what is practical. It is suspicious, even dismissive, of utopian fantasies, and the point of view repeatedly asserted is that human beings seeking utopias are likely to end up in dystopias. In fact, conservatives would take the position that perfection cannot be achieved by individuals or societies. We must necessarily be satisfied with modest improvements, but improvements nevertheless, not regressions. The Scottish philosopher David Hume articulated this sense of empiricism and combined it with a consistent anti-utopian position. He and his compatriot Adam Smith were great believers in the ongoing improvement of human society, ideas which the contemporary philosophers Steven Pinker and Yuval Noah Harari have subscribed to.

The conservative position is that improvements have to be gradual, and preferably peaceful. Sudden, violent attempts at so-called improvements are viewed with suspicion, because they are likely to backfire, destroy much of the good in the past and the present, and deliver a situation substantially worse than the earlier one. A philosophical approach involving the acceptance of the inevitability of violence is also resented by conservatives, on both moral and practical grounds. Conservatives have as their primary concern the freedom and well-being of individuals. Freely formed and voluntary, organic associative institutions are viewed positively while state-sponsored collectives are often viewed as inimical to individual interests.

~

Modern conservatism as a school of social and political philosophy is usually dated back to the politician and writer Edmund Burke. Conservatives borrowed heavily from other British and American thinkers such as Thomas Hobbes, John Locke, Adam Smith, David Hume, James Madison and Alexander Hamilton, thus giving much weightage to Anglo-Saxon thinkers and traditions. The idea that conservative thinking is frozen in time or calls to mind a golden past is a caricature presented by its opponents. Conservatism has evolved and there have been intense debates among people who describe themselves, or are externally described, as conservatives. The conservative tradition in Britain has come down from political practitioners like Robert Peel and the celebrated Benjamin Disraeli all the way to Margaret Thatcher. The best-known conservative philosopher in Britain today is Roger Scruton, who harks back not only to his worthy intellectual forebear Edmund Burke, but is also part of a continuing thread of intellectual connections that include Henry Maine – who studied the evolution of laws and legal systems – and F.W. Maitland – whose magisterial history of English common law is a brilliant conservative tract by itself.

Conservatives do not advocate anarchist or extreme libertarian positions. On the contrary, they attach a great deal of importance to horizontal social cohesion within limited geographies such as villages, towns or countries. The best articulation of this idea of voluntary, mutual bonding of people is found in literature, and comes from the finest of Anglo-Saxon writers. In *Henry V*, Shakespeare has young King Harry tell the assembled soldiers before the battle of Agincourt that all the members of the English army, which included aristocratic lords and yeomen peasants, were in fact part of the king's 'band of brothers'. Even if some of the men present on the battlefield were conscripted, Henry treats them as volunteers, emphasizing the free association of free individuals. We are confronted with a strong English state that gains its strength from a shared social and political vision. This vision is further elaborated upon by Scruton when he talks about 'the shared public realm of mutual loyalty', and it is the same vision that the French political thinker Alexis de Tocqueville refers to when he describes New England town meetings of all citizens.

It must be added that for conservatives the idea of a 'band of brothers' does not imply a levelling mediocre equality that socialists love. It refers to a shared solidarity across different, distinct persons, bound by mutual loyalty. For religious conservatives, equality is in the eyes of God and of the law; and for those who are not that religious, it is in the eyes of the law only. Conservatives emphasize that shared loyalty is required not in order to restrict individual freedom, but in order to give that freedom greater salience and meaning.

Despite not being utopian in its claims, conservatism has a universal quality to it. There are conservatives in all countries, societies and spheres. While the origin of the modern political doctrine of conservatism has a distinctly Anglo-Saxon flavour to it, one can argue that the roots of conservative thinking go back in the Western canon all the way to Plato, Aristotle, Isaiah and the Gospels.

~

This by no means makes conservatism in India purely or entirely an imported intellectual conceit. Its antecedents are both universal and Indian. Two of our civilization's foundational texts, the Shanti Parva of the Mahabharata and the Tirukkural of Tiruvalluvar, can be seen as providing the enduring basis of Indian conservatism. Kautilya too has conservative credentials. While dealing with the gradual emergence of a new humanism, the great

Telugu poet Allasami Peddanna, who was a luminary at the court of the sixteenth-century Vijayanagara emperor Krishna Deva Raya, dealt with concerns that are uncannily similar to those of Scruton. Peddanna wrestled with the relationship of the individual to inherited traditions while maintaining human agency, which refers to the individual's ability not to be imprisoned by traditions but to be able to change them in a sober manner. Allasami addresses this core conservative concern with refreshing panache, some five hundred years before Scruton.

The Mahabharata and the Tirukkural deal with the three pursuits of humankind: artha or economic and political activity, kama or the pursuit of passion and beauty, and dharma or the pursuit of virtue and morality. The fourth pursuit, moksha or salvation, presumably the most important, is automatically dealt with if the first three are addressed.

The discussions on dharma focus on three important ideas: Samskaras or character traits, which can also be read as Charitra, Raja Dharma and Sukshma Dharma. Charitra refers to character – of individuals, of groups and of the sovereign. Individuals are required to focus on their duties and obligations prior to seeking rights. Mahatma Gandhi was of the opinion that when duties are performed properly, rights follow automatically. Groups of individuals are expected to live together peacefully and to transact with each other in a trustworthy manner.

Raja Dharma, or the appropriate virtuous conduct of a king, is repeatedly described as that which promotes the happiness of his subjects. The sovereign is required to have a good character and not derive joy from tyranny. Kalidasa's *Raghuvamsha* depicts with great sorrow the tragedy of a land with an evil king. It is almost as if the Indic sages anticipate Jefferson's position in the American Declaration of Independence that the state needs to create an atmosphere where individuals can pursue happiness. To some extent, Raja Dharma anticipates the medieval English Magna Carta, or Great Charter, which is seen by many scholars as the first attempt to make the king too abide by the law. The propounders of the concept of Raja Dharma are remarkably similar to the authors of the Magna Carta in suggesting that the sovereign is not above the law. Raja Dharma requires that individuals be protected – an obvious forerunner to the Jeffersonian idea of protecting life and liberty, which along with the right to pursue happiness constitutes the famous tripod so often quoted from the American Declaration of Independence. The sovereign is required to act in a manner that prevents the emergence of Matsya Nyaya or the situation where the big fish eat the small.

Nothing is more horrifying than Matsya Nyaya for ancient Indian thinkers. A state that protects is key, and this implies that the state itself is not predatory. This idea is elaborated on by Maitland, who places it within the traditions of English common law. Raja Dharma would require the sovereign to maintain 'domestic tranquillity', an objective echoed by the American founding fathers in their Constitution. It would require the sovereign to protect the life and property of the citizens. The question of the state expropriating property is vigorously negated in the *Isavasya Upanishad*, which explicitly forbids the coveting of another's wealth, a maxim which applies to kings and commoners equally.

Sukshma Dharma talks about the appropriate response to situations where trade-offs are required, when creative tension is experienced between conflicting actions which appear equally virtuous. The answers are never easy. But the Indic texts are clear: one cannot avoid these questions because they are difficult. Tiruvalluvar is most emphatic that the answers must pass the test of practical empiricism.

Another concept I will frequently refer to is Yuga Dharma, which goes back some two and a half millennia. Yuga Dharma suggests that correct conduct changes with time. Yuga means epoch or time period. Each yuga requires different responses from the virtuous.

The parallels between these robust Indic traditions and Anglo-Saxon conservatism can be seen as accidental or as examples of human synchronicity.

~

Let us switch gears and consider names associated with modern Indian conservatism, focusing for the time being on the pre-Independence era. The first is Rammohun Roy, who was a political conservative and a supporter of British rule, while being a social and religious reformer – a reformer and not a radical. The second is Bankim Chandra Chatterjee, who can be characterized as almost the founder of Hindu conservatism. It is Bankim who ensured that Hindu nationalism had intellectual respectability as a positive and credible point of view. Bankim was also among the first to articulate a Hindu identity in contemporary language. He borrowed from Sanskritic sources and wove into them strands that made sense in the language of his times. This is a characteristic conservative exercise.

A frequently asked question is whether Hindu nationalism, by its very Hindu and very nationalistic nature, can be a branch of conservatism at all. This needs to be viewed contextually. Abraham Lincoln, who was perhaps the greatest American president, referred to the 'mystic chords of memory' that bind people together. When you combine this with the fact that the British conquered India and pretty openly took the position that they had conquered it from predominantly Muslim rulers, it becomes clear that non-Muslims in India – taking into account that the very term 'Hindu' was an evolving one – had no option but to seek a renaissance if they were to sustain themselves as a community, with shared mutual loyalty, rather than as atomized splinters. Bankim and Lajpat Rai along with several others realized that a shared Hindu cultural identity could be the basis of overcoming vertical and horizontal boundaries among Hindus, like caste. They could then be a 'band of brothers'. Therein lies the origin of seeking an imagined Hindu identity in the mode that has been so well articulated by the American scholar Benedict Anderson, who has ably analysed modern nationalisms. This Hindu identity acknowledges the myriad diversities present inside that construct. A renaissance, as against a brand-new identity, implies that the mystic chord of memory is an enduring one, even if there have been major political and social discontinuities over time. To dismiss this approach as reactionary is less than fair. It is a branch of conservatism, even if it sought substantive change from the prevalent circumstances of its times.

Bankim was less sanguine about British rule than Rammohun Roy. But he too was a supporter of British rule insofar as he made the argument that British rule was providential for Hindus in helping ignite a Hindu revival and renaissance. Swami Vivekananda too shared the view that the association with the British was a providential opportunity for Hindus. Vivekananda included Muslims and Christians within an Indian cultural rubric, acknowledging that both for historical and for demographic reasons, this Indian culture would have a large dose of a Hindu character. Arguably, there is nothing inherently illegitimate or undemocratic about such a position. Scruton would argue that respecting the majority culture does not imply support for majoritarian positions. And given Indian diversities, which we will presently discuss, the majority culture emerges as a benign rainbow rather than as a threatening 'kultur', the German word that has acquired nasty connotations because the Nazis loved it.

In economics, the pre-Independence era conservative thinkers include Dadabhai Naoroji and Romesh Chunder Dutt. Historians of this period who can be classified as conservatives include Jadunath Sarkar, Radha Kumud Mukherjee, K.M. Munshi, R.C. Majumdar, D.B. Parasnis, G.S. Sardesai and Nilakanta Sastri.

The brilliant contemporary historian Dipesh Chakravarti, who can by no means be classified as a conservative, has incisively analysed Jadunath Sarkar's views on character and its role in determining historical destiny. As it turns out, Sarkar in the early twentieth century was following in the intellectual footsteps of ancient Indian thinkers who emphasized 'samskaras' and 'charitra'. Surendranath Dasgupta, M. Hiriyanna and Sarvepalli Radhakrishnan brought the conservative perspective to philosophical studies in India. All three were historians of Indian philosophy who simultaneously came up with positions of their own that have become part of our enduring and continuing traditions. The great sociologist G.S. Ghurye, who began his work before 1947 and went on for quite a bit after that, was definitely a conservative. He was concerned about organic processes within India that led to gradual change and the resulting creation of a civilized society. In the field of aesthetics, the best-known conservative thinker of that era was Ananda K. Coomaraswamy.

In the post-1885 period, as the Indian National Congress grew in prominence, the most important conservative political figure to emerge was Gopal Krishna Gokhale. Under his leadership, the Congress was committed to debate, discussion and negotiation, working for gradual, evolutionary, constitutional political change. Social activists like Mahadev Govind Ranade and Maharshi D.K. Karve were deeply concerned that excessive focus on political change without any social change could end up being counterproductive. They were advocates of social change through discussion, legislation, persuasion and example.

A similar impulse on the economic, scientific and technological sides drove the pioneering industrialist J.N. Tata. Tata was concerned about human capital in India. In his celebrated letter to Gokhale, he laments the fact that the colonial education system produced too many lawyers and not enough scientists, engineers and practical persons. In this regard, he was following in the footsteps of his fellow citizen of Bombay, the renowned Jagannath Sunkersett, who had similar concerns in the area of education and worked actively with Governor Elphinstone to encourage education in the then Bombay Presidency.

Concerns about education and social change, oddly enough, were very important to persons who may not completely fit the conservative label – Iyothee Thass, Jyotiba Phule, Cornelia Sorabji, Pandita Ramabai Ranade, Behramji Malabari and E.V. Ramaswamy Naicker, all of whom supported the continuance of British rule, at least until Indian education levels were higher and Indian society had comprehensively embraced principles of individualism and meritocracy.

Individualism – emphasis on individual human effort – which is meant to trump the tyranny of collective identities while not disregarding the inherited wisdom of communities, remains one of those fine balancing act arguments that conservative philosophers love to participate in. This focus on individual effort is also sometimes referred to as focus on human agency, where the individual actively accepts responsibility for her actions. Such an approach ensures that collective victimhood, collective entitlements without appropriate action on the part of individuals and communities themselves, grievance-mongering as well as entrenched non-meritocratic hierarchies tend to be looked down upon by conservatives. It is important to note that Jyotiba Phule worked with another conservative scholar, R.G. Bhandarkar, to set up schools and institutions rather than succumb to the temptation of sloganeering and the culture of constantly seeking handouts.

Support for, or at least acceptance of, the beneficial aspects of British rule, clearly a modest conservative position, arose from different motivations. Scholars like Narmadashankar Dave and Bhau Daji Lad saw opportunities in British rule at a particular point in time in Indian history. Gokhale faced opposition for his moderate politics even when he lived. After his death, the Congress under Gandhi's leadership reduced its emphasis on constitutional change, but embraced the distaste for violent change with even greater gusto.

Sir Syed Ahmad Khan's views were almost a mirror image of Bankim's. He felt that British rule was providential for India's Muslims and protected them from the tyranny of the majority. In pointedly encouraging Shia enrolment at Aligarh University, Sir Syed was clearly hoping to create a 'band of brothers' among India's Muslims. This is also the reason Aligarh tried to encourage Urdu as a common binding force among Indian Muslims. In this atmosphere, the Gujarati Muslim Badruddin Tyabji forced his entire family to switch to Urdu.

The question that pops up is whether the 'band of brothers' phenomenon can extend horizontally across both Hindus and Muslims. This of course has been a question that has continuously haunted all discussions and debates in modern India. It should not be easily dismissed. During the 1857 uprising, there was an element of brotherhood among Hindu and Muslim sepoys who fought to defend their dharma and their din, as the historian Rudrangshu Mukherjee brilliantly points out. They even chose a common titular leader in the aged emperor in Delhi. We will discuss this further in the section on politics.

Pherozeshah Mehta, Badruddin Tyabji, Lajpat Rai,

Madan Mohan Malaviya and Sivaswamy Aiyar in their own ways represented different aspects of conservative politics in the pre-Gandhi era. Tej Bahadur Sapru, Sankaran Nair, M.R. Jayakar and Srinivasa Sastri distanced themselves from Gandhi's extraconstitutional methods. These individuals, along with Ramaswamy Mudaliar and Shanmukham Chetty (the intellectual heavyweights of the Justice Party), the journalist Frank Moraes and Shyamaprasad Mukherjee of the Hindu Mahasabha can be viewed as bedrock political conservatives.

Meanwhile, a conservative caucus developed within Gandhi's Congress. This group was particularly suspicious of the leftist tendencies of Subhas Chandra Bose and Jawaharlal Nehru as well as those of the new-formed Congress Socialist Party, which included figures like Jayaprakash Narayan. This conservative caucus within the Congress included Rajendra Prasad, Vallabhbhai Patel, G.B. Pant, C. Rajagopalachari, G. Bordoloi, Pattabhi Sitaramayya and B.C. Roy among others.

In the princely states, several important political conservatives emerged. They included the visionary M. Visweswarayya, who began his career in British India and then moved to the state of Mysore; the brilliant M.A. Sreenivasan, who started his career in Mysore state and went on to become the prime minister of Gwalior; the sober and energetic Mirza Ismail, who had a long tenure as the prime minister of Mysore, followed by stints as the prime minister of Jaipur and Hyderabad; as well as the eccentric and controversial C.P. Ramaswami Aiyar, one of the most brilliant lawyers of British India, who went on to become the prime minister of Travancore state.

While talking of two seminal and important figures in modern India, Mahatma Gandhi and Dr Bhimrao Ambedkar, the question of whether they were conservatives arises. Gandhi disdained violence and virtually expelled Bose from the Congress party for preaching revolutionary violent action among other things. So while there are conservative elements in Gandhi's thinking, I do not want to make a claim to conservative ownership of Gandhi as this would ensure that the debate gets hijacked into this sphere, and that other aspects of the argument are ignored. I cannot, however, resist the temptation to point out that many leftist academics in fact do argue that the Mahatma was a conservative! This argument of the leftists should of course be a source of considerable amusement for us conservatives. Ambedkar is equally problematic. Politically he was a conservative, supporting British rule right through the Quit India days. He was also a thorough constitutionalist. Again, if I claim him as one of our own, with some legitimate grounds, the discussion will get sidetracked. Let us leave this aside for the moment.

The same is the case with Jyotiba Phule and Ramaswamy Naicker, both political conservatives who supported British rule but who were radical in their social vision. I think it would be wise if no one tried to claim these brilliant and enigmatic individuals in their entirety.

The Hindu Mahasabha leaders V.D. Savarkar and B.S. Moonje can be seen as building on the foundations of Hindu nationalism that had been laid by Bankim and enhanced by Lajpat Rai. Savarkar coined the expression 'Hindutva', which can be seen as a conservative or as a radical term, depending on the lens you are wearing. K.B. Hedgewar was the founder of the Rashtriya Swayamsevak Sangh (RSS), a distinctly conservative social and cultural organization with political affiliations. M.S. Golwalkar took forward the work begun by Hedgewar. Later, Deendayal Upadhyaya emerged as the ideologue of an Indic political doctrine, which to this day provides inspiration for the politics of Hindu nationalism. Where do Savarkar, Moonje, Hedgewar, Golwalkar and Upadhyaya, all of whom can be aptly described as Hindu nationalists, fit in when we are talking about Indian conservatism in the political arena? In my opinion, and I am not shy about saying this, Hindu nationalism is either a valid and legitimate subset of Indian conservatism or a movement which has significant overlaps with Indian conservatism. The development of this intellectual lineage will be dealt with later.

You might note that I have excluded from my list both the Urdu poet and politician Muhammad Iqbal (widely regarded as the inspiration behind the Pakistan movement) and the Tamil scholar Maraimalai Adigal, who were interested in altering current paradigms in order to fit into one of a glory associated with the distant past. Their search had less of the elements of the renaissance spirit and more of a reactionary tone. They both also had separatist lenses through which they viewed India. Given that sobriety demanded that the British contribution of imposing political unity on India was on balance a positive one, separatism can hardly be accepted as conservative in its spirit. Jinnah, while starting as a conservative, ended up resembling an extremist. During the French Revolution, extremists of the Jinnah variety were referred to as Jacobins. To give up the benefits of two centuries of gradual evolution of Indian political unity and to opt for abrupt surgery is not something that conservatives can appreciate.

Conservatism is fluid, empirical and local in its manifestations, despite its universalist basis. Americans are still arguing whether President Lincoln was a conservative. A hundred years from now, we will still be arguing this matter about Gandhi and Ambedkar. I am of course tempted to respectfully avoid talking about Nehru, a self-proclaimed anti-conservative. But that would be a mistake. I need to acknowledge that on many occasions I find his quotations useful. I must assume, therefore, that there were sensible, sensitive and doubtless conservative parts to him. Subhas Chandra Bose is more difficult. He did not write much. He certainly had a link with Vivekananda and Bengali Hindu revivalism. But in some sense he was the archetypal leftist 'Jacobin', imbued with a fiery idealism that is conducive to charisma, something that conservatives distrust.

~

Balanced with its universalist flavour is the fact that conservatism is biased towards the local, the patriotic, the national. The summary argument would be that 'conservatism is opposed to a universalist ideology, even as its impulse is universal'. (I would like to take credit for that argument. But I need to acknowledge that it was in fact made by my son Vijay during one of our conversations when we were trying to paraphrase the central features of conservatism.) In general, we conservatives do not hold that there are universal solutions possible for all societies or countries. We believe that each society will have to develop institutions and processes that are directly related to the history, geography, traditions and culture of that individual unit.

This does not mean that we can compromise with the principle of the supremacy of the individual and her freedom and responsibility to think and act on her own, which we need to remember appeared 'self-evident' to Jefferson, and rightly so. A society that does not meet this test fails in the eyes of conservatives. This of course implies that there are good and better societies and good and better polities as opposed to those that are bad and worse. The Soviet Union, Communist China, Nazi Germany, contemporary Saudi Arabia and Iran are, quite simply speaking, on the bad end of the spectrum, while Western democracies and India are at the better end of the spectrum, but please note that they are by no means perfect. While pursuing the perfection that tyrants seek, relative imperfection is always seen as better than ending up with the bad. Given our belief in the impossibility of perfection, we are forever on the road of gradual improvements that heads towards that impossible destination. The US founding fathers had it right when they wrote in their Constitution about the search for 'a more perfect union', not 'the perfect union'.

The view that conservatives love the old and oppose all change is both simplistic and wrong. Conservatives are most certainly not reactionaries. We only love those parts of the old and inherited that are constructive and creative and not dysfunctional. We are committed to change, which as the Greek philosopher Heraclitus observed, and as the *Yajur Veda* articulates, is inevitable. We, however, do not believe in jettisoning features of the past that are worth preserving or that we feel are worth cherishing.

In our view, the principal challenge faced by societies is how to change constructively, without losing things of value in the process of change. Therefore, in principle, we are opposed to revolutionary change, preferring the evolutionary variety any day. When confronted with arguments that everything needs to be pulled down, we are both amused and horrified.

In political terms, the French Revolution, in our opinion, serves as a good example of the folly of revolution. About the so-called glorious October Revolution of the Bolsheviks, the less said the better. One must grudgingly admire the communists. They managed to imitate the worst features of Tsarist Russia and they brought to their imitative efforts a level of ruthless efficiency, which the flabby tsars could not have ever pulled off. Movements like these almost invariably result in a reign of terror, and social and political institutions that have outlived their time and need change are replaced with caricatures of the constructive.

There are times, however, when powerful forces in society fail to understand and appreciate the requirement for evolutionary change. The stubborn unwillingness of the leadership of the American South to accept the need to abolish the institution of slavery resulted in war becoming the instrument of that change. However, such change induced by violence almost always results in a bitter aftermath and wounds that do not get healed for generations, as was the case in the American South. The contrast with the state of New York, where the conservative Alexander Hamilton was able to persuade slave owners to be sensible and accept compensation for giving up their slaves, is a fascinating one. New York does not suffer from the bitterness that still plagues the American South. The bitter legacy of the French Revolution lasted for a long, long time. Some would argue that after two and a half centuries, it is yet to disappear.

Conservatives are acutely aware that love for the particular, the community, the society, the country, can sometimes develop along pathological lines. This was the problem with extreme Slavophile intellectuals in Russia, who believed that a love for Mother Russia must be accompanied by the ancient prejudice against Jews; and a problem as well with the Romantics in France, who distorted their love of mystic memories and the 'band of brothers' by polluting it with the taint of anti-Semitism, when they joined the anti-Dreyfus movement launched against an innocent Jewish army officer, Alfred Dreyfus, who was imprisoned as a spy on flimsy, concocted evidence.

The great Japanese thinker Fukuzawa provided a fine foundation for embracing change with continuity as Japan embarked on its Meiji era. Sadly, abandoning Fukuzawa's sober conservatism and opting for shrill demagogue voices brought Japan to an unfortunate denouement, as the Japanese took to aggressive militarism which resulted in their violent defeat in 1945.

The ultimate caricature of conservatism, which incidentally was stoutly opposed by many conservatives, was seen in the twentieth century in Nazi Germany. But no philosophy or doctrine can and should be judged by its pathological aberrations. The German concept of 'heimat', or homeland, comes through as a tender expression in the opera *Tristram und Isolde*. Rabindranath Tagore captures the idea of intense affection for a distant heimat when his character, the Kabuliwala, thinks of his native Afghanistan. The Nazis took the concept of love for one's homeland as implying contempt for other lands. They practised a similar distortion with the expression 'volk', or people, and introduced the expression 'herrenvolk', or master race. There was no longer an emphasis on loving one's 'band of brothers'. Instead, the emphasis was on asserting superiority over other people. The consequences of these linguistic distortions were not harmless. They ended up being catastrophic for Germany.

It would be easy for us to feel comfortably sanctimonious that India is the only country in the world without a tradition of anti-Semitism. We may have been nice to Jews, but how have we dealt with different 'others'? Extreme pathological nationalism usually involves not just love for one's country and one's people, but also a hatred for the 'other'. It is not the case that the pathological possibilities of extreme nationalism or even subnationalism are restricted to foreign lands. We have witnessed this in our own country even within the last hundred years. Mahatma Gandhi's Khilafat movement was an attempt to establish a 'band of brothers' feeling that included Hindus and Muslims. In Malabar, among other places, it backfired. Instead of a joint Muslim– Hindu political movement against the British, the Moplah movement (Moplah 'rebellion' according to the British) in Malabar attacked not the British Raj, but the Hindu 'other' and involved horrific instances of murder, rape and forced conversion. Extremist Hindu ideologues and, for that matter, Sikh ideologues have not been far behind in 'othering' Muslims. The twentieth century is littered with names of places that can only horrify us: Kohat, Kanpur, Rawalpindi, Calcutta, Noakhali, Nagpur, Lahore, Garhmukteshwar, Jabalpur, Ahmedabad,

Moradabad, Malliana, Meerut, Delhi, Bhagalpur, Samastipur, Godhra, Bhiwandi, Jalgaon, Bombay – the list is so long that one has to hang one's head in shame and admit that our pretence of moral superiority over German hyper-nationalists is pretty weak and unconvincing.

The publicity given to Hindu–Muslim and Sikh–Muslim 'othering' before 1947 and to Hindu–Muslim othering after 1947 sometimes misses out on various subnational othering attempts. The selective killing of Hindu bus travellers by Khalistani elements; the targeting of a whole aircraft, Air India's Kanishka, by Khalistani subnationalists based in Canada; and the state-supported othering of Sikhs in our capital city in 1984 are shameful events that are difficult to erase from our collective memory. Subnational pathologies can be very violent and vicious. One only needs to talk to 'outsiders' who lived in Shillong for decades or to exiled Kashmiri Pandits who were forced out of their ancient homeland. On a smaller scale, there remain movements and incidents to remind us that there is a bit of the Nazi in many Indians. The attacks on Madrasis and Biharis in Mumbai, the attacks on Tamils in Bangalore during the Kaveri riots, the attacks on Bengalis in Assam, the attacks by Naga groups on Meiteis in some districts of Manipur – all of these contain the seeds of pathological poison. It is easy for a 'band of brothers' to turn into a band of murderers, and our country stands out as an unhappy laboratory for testing out murderous pathologies. Needless to say, even as we advocate the creation of horizontal solidarities, conservatives must remain ever watchful and vigilant that 'othering' does not become the rule. The violent outcomes of such othering must make good conservatives shudder. In this context, Hindu nationalist ideologues are often tempted to go in for a systematic 'othering' of the Muslim. This is an approach of unmitigated folly.

~

Conservatives tend to be supporters of market-based solutions in the economic sphere. The market where people meet, negotiate and transact is an ancient human institution that has organically developed in different societies. It requires the voluntary acquiescence of individuals, who are so dear to conservatives. It does not involve forceful interventions by any tyrant. It mandates easy entry and exit, almost exuding the spirit of liberty in that process. It is remarkably peaceful and peaceable in its conduct. It is based on trust among participants and enhances the factor of trust, which is such a key lubricant in human intercourse. Contemporary leftist criticism of markets tends to focus quite hysterically on the mistaken notion that the market is invariably dominated by 'exploitative monopolists', without bothering to understand that defenders of markets are usually the strongest opponents of monopolistic practices.

In the cultural sphere, conservatives tend to be committed, even obsessive, lovers of tradition and heritage. The great cultural achievements of our forebears – be it the architecture of our temples, the music of peerless ragas or the brilliance of our poetic traditions – are always to be treated with respect and many times with wonderment. Contemporary cultural creations are seen as being a part of an enduring tradition. The Anglo-American poet T.S. Eliot, a seminal figure in the conservative pantheon, has emphasized that art which ignores tradition ends up becoming sterile. The prolific music composer S.D. Burman articulated this point very well when he positioned his own modern music as organically linked to both the classical and folk traditions of our country.

In the social sphere, conservatives attach great importance to institutions like the family, which may actually have its advantages in our evolutionary biology and which has been time-tested in many societies we consider admirable. We also have a fondness for voluntary associations like the sports club, the trade guild, the chamber of commerce, the bhajan mandali, the sangeet sabha and so on, which have evolved organically to become important institutions. We are aware that these institutions can atrophy and thus require frequent regeneration through constructive change. Changing the bathwater is completely in order, as long as the baby is safe.

In political matters, we conservatives are always for gradual, constitutional change and are opposed to breakneck revolutionary change. And we are always on the watch as to whether the proposed change enhances individual freedoms or curtails them.

In the aesthetic realm, we have a preference for traditional patterns and styles. We believe that these have evolved over time, keeping in mind the needs and sensitivities of generations gone past, and that itself makes them worth being taken seriously.

~

My friend Ram Guha has raised an important question, which one cannot run away from. After all, empiricism, support for incremental change and rejection of utopias can be seen as core principles of liberalism. What, then, is the difference between conservatism and liberalism? To my mind, the single biggest distinction lies in the difference in thinking between the English philosopher Hobbes and the French philosopher Rousseau. Hobbes believed all of civilization was an attempt by humans to gradually move from their brutish beginnings to a better, but not necessarily perfect, present. In Indic terms, the proper practice of artha and dharma takes us away from the dreaded reign of Matsya Nyaya, when brute power prevails and the big fish eat the small ones. Rousseau believed all of civilization represents social oppression that attempts to imprison primitive humans who are inherently noble. Liberals, therefore, tend to attack traditions and customs. Many of them would find the concept of a 'band of brothers' inherently oppressive. It is true that liberals, unlike totalitarians, favour incremental change. But they derive the desired direction of change from theoretical abstractions like utility, common good and so on, and not from lived reality. Hence their disdain for the wisdom of the common swain, which is the expression Burke uses for common peasant farmers. The theoretically well-armed liberal savant thinks he knows what is best for the swain!

Conservatives invariably believe that not only do we not know what is best for anyone, but also that tampering with inherited wisdom can be dangerous. Liberals, despite not advocating violence and the immediate establishment of a revolutionary state, are in fact utopian in their goals. They believe human beings have created human problems, and if we pass laws and set up institutions these problems can be solved. Conservatives believe that many, perhaps most, human problems are inherent to our predicament and destiny. Tinkering can at best ameliorate bits and pieces, and some kinds of tinkering may make things worse.

Starting with their founding guru Rousseau, liberals have a profound sense of grievance against society, against the way humans have organized themselves until now. This is the reason liberals are found at the forefront of all movements based on victimhood and grievance-mongering. The support given by both liberals and conservatives for markets is an overlap which is particularly prone to misunderstanding. Liberals favour markets because they work or can be made to work to pursue liberal goals. If tomorrow it can be shown that central planning works better at reducing inequalities or in empowering select minorities, which are typical liberal goals, their attachment to markets will disappear. Conservatives will continue to oppose central planning as essentially immoral and undesirable. Markets are organic, evolved, voluntary human endeavours. Central planning is imposed and involuntary. It is a violation of Raja Dharma in Indic terms, and of the rights to liberty and private property in Anglo-Saxon terms.

In recent times, we find many persons who call themselves liberals abandoning their emphasis on the individual and opting for the protection of group identities, especially where these groups are seen as 'oppressed'. The focus on encouraging victimhood among Dalits as a group without corresponding sympathy or support for individual Dalits is an example of this approach. This has resulted in a perverse distortion of liberalism. This effort contrasts completely with King Henry V's attempt to create a 'band of brothers' feeling across lords and peasants. It starts with the hard hypothesis that peasants and aristocrats can never be members of the same band. It goes on to argue that gay peasants and female aristocrats are subgroups that need hand-holding, especially against hegemons who can be white and male in the West and upper caste and male in India. Liberal thinkers are often seduced into this sinister trap.

Conservatives know better. These artificial group identities are imagined and created precisely in order to destroy traditions. Too often, persons of the liberal persuasion seem to like change as an end in itself because they are so unhappy with the present. Conservatives on the other hand are clear that change is needed to conserve the best in our past. We simply will not part with precious legacies passed on to us by dead white males or by dead upper-caste males, viewing them only through the lens of power and oppression, even if it has an element of that. We will alter, we will change, but we will not completely abandon.

One can round it off by going back to the well-known conservative position that we are part of a contract not only among the living, but also with our ancestors and the generations yet to come. We are trustees of this earth and of the better parts of those things handed to us by our ancestors as we pass these precious trusts on to our children and theirs. While there are conservatives who are simultaneously atheists, it is true that most conservatives have a soft spot for religion, both from the practical consideration that religion tends to provide the most stable bedrock for ethical commerce among individuals, and from the insight that the religious engagements of our ancestors represent some of the finest parts of our human inheritance.

I hope to end this book with a conclusion that I will state in advance, so that it stays in your mind as you read the rest of my verbiage in alternate moods of boredom, exasperation and, I hope, interest. Quite simply speaking, conservatism as a philosophy spanning various realms of human endeavour – the economic, the cultural, the social, the political and the aesthetic – has an extraordinarily important contribution to make, a contribution which has not received sufficient academic or public attention in recent times in India. It might hold many answers, even if imperfect, to engaging with and dealing with the numerous conundrums of our perilous times, and perhaps the even more perilous times ahead.

Let us now proceed to examine Indian conservatism in five areas, with a focus on the intellectual and practical concerns of the recent past and the present.

1

Modern Indian Conservatism in the Economic Sphere

The Indian conservative position in the economic sphere goes back to Dadabhai Naoroji and R.C. Dutt, who were of the opinion that the inimical effects of colonial rule were not a result of the British government in London, Calcutta and Simla practising laissez-faire, but because it actively intervened to distort the markets in goods, services and factors to help Britain at the expense of India. The Viceroy in Calcutta felt it was inappropriate to get involved when famine struck large parts of India as this would violate principles of free trade and free enterprise. Naoroji and Dutt pointed out that the same Viceroy and his Council were willing to impose tariffs that discriminated in favour of British exports to India, maintain an artificial exchange rate that tilted surpluses towards Britain, grant support to British-owned monopolies and oligopolies while denying the same to Indian entrepreneurs, subvert Indian infrastructure like railways, transcontinental cables and so on, not with commercial purposes in mind, but for imperial strategic reasons and almost invariably at a disproportionate cost to Indian taxpayers.

During the First World War, Indian suppliers were subject to price controls and had to sell war material to the Allies at a fraction of market prices. American businesses, which were protected by their free government, did not suffer from this handicap. Both Naoroji and Dutt held firm that the Indian entrepreneur, the Indian merchant, the Indian producer did not need or want any special support. What they advocated was a free and level playing field where British economic interests and the interests of favoured British crony capitalists would not be the deciding factor in the framing of government policies and actions.

It is important to remember that Burke and the Scottish philosopher and 'father of economics' Adam Smith had in their time, for similar reasons, opposed the East India Company which was determinedly tyrannical and mercantilist in serving its own interests over those of India and Indians. Burke was opposed to the blithe assumption that there was nothing valuable in the traditions Indians had developed over millennia, and that a mere commercial organization with dubious morals could be allowed to ride roughshod over India. He was also correct in his analysis that such a situation would corrode British politics and society, too. Adam Smith was dead against granting political power to a commercial organization, which he predicted was bound to misuse such power. He was also opposed to all monopolists, and the East India Company in the late eighteenth century was an egregious monopolist. In their defence of free markets and damning of monopolistic exploitation, Naoroji and Dutt ended up as eloquent intellectual descendants of Adam Smith.

The Naoroji–Dutt tradition in economic thinking was carried forward in independent India by B.R. Shenoy. He repeatedly warned about distortions in the economy caused by state action, although now it was not being imposed by a foreign occupier but by a home-grown state that was committed to top-down planning and the pursuit of a statist industrial policy, even if it was at the cost of large sections of the country, including farmers, private entrepreneurs with minimal political connections and so on. Shenoy did receive support from Swatantra Party political figures like C. Rajagopalachari, Minoo Masani, the Raja of Ramgarh, N. Dandekar, N.G. Ranga and

M. Ruthnaswamy, and from a few businesspersons like A.D. Shroff and Viren Shah. Most Indian businesspersons preferred to make deals with the state apparatus rather than demand freedom in the tradition of Naoroji and Dutt. Shenoy and his handful of like-minded colleagues comprehensively lost the battle.

Indian economics professionals in Delhi, Calcutta, Trivandrum and Madras only differed from each other in how extreme they were in their demands for state intervention and control. In Bombay and Poona, the saner voices of P.R. Brahmananda, C.N. Vakil, D.R. Gadgil and V.M. Dandekar tried to persuade our political leaders to retain a sense of balance. Unfortunately, they too were not successful.

~

The statist economic policies of India, implemented soon after Independence, became entrenched after the infamous Avadi session of the Congress party in 1955. From a consequential careerist perspective, it made sense for economists to embrace the prevailing political fashions. This ensured promotions at the Delhi School of Economics and at the Indian Statistical Institute, apart from sinecures in the Planning Commission and miscellaneous committees, and of course invitations to foreign boondoggles. Many have argued that these economists were not intellectually compromised – they were simply part of the prevailing zeitgeist. I think it is important to note at least in passing that these leftists were, in their personal lives, trying to get the best deals they could. In this context, they resembled the very people they opposed – the selfish individuals who were pursuing their private profits. That, of course, is one of the enduring ironies of our history.

It is to the credit of the Swatantra Party politicians that most were true conservatives. They did point out the damage done by dirigiste economic policies in ensuring that India and Indians remain poor even as other countries, particularly countries to our east, became wealthier. But they were not merely objecting to the bad consequences of these policies. In philosophical terms, this would be called 'consequentialism', where you object to some actions because they result in bad outcomes. As genuine moralists, conservatives had to take up a moral position about something being undesirable, irrespective of the outcomes or 'consequences'. Conservatives believed fervently in the centrality of the individual and not that of the commissar in Yojana Bhavan, the headquarters of the Planning Commission. They did, therefore, oppose central planning as a matter of principle, not just because they felt its results were harmful.

~

In the early 1950s, Rajagopalachari translated many sections of the Tirukkural, the ancient Tamil classic, into English. Tiruvalluvar, the author of this text, had focused on the three purusharthas or trivargas that are discussed extensively in the Shanti Parva of the Mahabharata as kama, artha and dharma – referred to in Tamil as inbam/kama, porul and aram. Going back to the earliest wellsprings of Indic tradition, Rajagopalachari was able to elegantly argue that the intrusive state that taxes too much and cramps individual initiative is not bad only because it is inefficient and does not work. It is bad also because it is immoral or, in our vocabulary, adharmic, lacking in righteousness.

Minoo Masani, an early socialist, was among thinkers like the English writer Stephen Spender, the African American writer Richard Wright and the European intellectual Arthur Koestler, who all understood the proclivities of the Bolshevik god who had failed. As a principled freedom lover and a relentless anti-communist, Masani saw that Indian planning needed to be opposed not only because it perpetuated poverty, but also because it represented the thin end of the wedge that would ultimately lead to the extinction of liberty.

As the reins were transferred from Pandit Nehru to his daughter after a short interregnum, this is pretty much what happened. Indira Gandhi surrounded herself with many hard-core crypto-Stalinists. It is possible that some of them were deliberate plants by the communists within the 'bourgeois democratic' Congress party. Some might have been KGB agents. In any event, the Indian state became more and more intrusive in the economic domain. The beneficiaries were political personages and crony capitalists rather than genuine entrepreneurs. India's position, as compared to other similar economies, deteriorated on virtually every relative scale.

This led to the first criticism of the Indian economic strategy. The simple argument was that the consequences of the choices made by India were bad. The economists Jagdish Bhagwati, Padma Desai and T.N. Srinivasan left India for positions in North American academia, where their empirical work was well received. They established that the Indian economic strategy was simply not working. In a quieter tone, Manmohan Singh too argued that the theory that India could not and should not try to increase its exports, which was known as 'export pessimism', was tied to our leftist anti-foreign trade position. It was in fact becoming self-fulfilling in India and needed revisiting.

The monetary economist C. Rangarajan argued that incessant inflation, which was embedded in socialist policy and practice, was extremely anti-poor. Even a UK Labour Party supporter like Meghnad Desai in Britain was able to perceive that statist India was headed in the wrong direction. However, none of these intellectual currents made a difference at Jawaharlal Nehru University (JNU) or Delhi University (DU), both of which remained – and, for that matter, remain – hostile to markets and subscribe to the fashionable leftist attack on a new straw man called neo-liberalism. 'Neo-liberalism' was and still is the expression used by left-wing academics to describe the shift towards free market ideas that happened in Britain and America under Margaret Thatcher and Ronald Reagan. That doctrine has since spread around much of the world.

~

History, however, overtook intellectual fashions. The Berlin Wall fell, the Soviet Union collapsed and India was faced with multiple crises characterized by high inflation, low growth, dwindling foreign trade and an impossible balance of payments situation. Willy-nilly, India adopted some aspects of so-called neo-liberalism – lower tariffs, fiscal discipline, elimination of an anti-export bias and so on – even if only in a half-hearted manner. Younger economists, many with one foot on foreign soil – Kaushik Basu, Arvind Panagariya, Raghuram Rajan, Arvind Subramanian and Surjit Bhalla – came up with a nuanced defence of markets, individual initiative and entrepreneurial freedom. But by and large, most of these attempts remained focused on the good and bad consequences of specific policies, as they were rooted in empirical studies trying to understand what works and what does not. Deepak Lal, also an exile in North America, has remained a brilliant intellectual descendant of Adam Smith, consistently defending the political and economic liberty of the individual and her right to be free from state tyranny, both as a moral necessity and as something that results in positive consequences.

~

Amartya Sen remains an interesting outlier. His attacks on states and societies which do not focus on the development of human capacities have been publicized. What has not received sufficient attention is his emphatic plea for liberating Indian entrepreneurship, and his arguments that while claiming to help the poor, many actions of the Indian state are in fact regressive in nature. Only the superficial student will conclude that Sen is a simple-minded statist or a fashionable critic of neo-liberalism, whatever that might mean.

The same can be said of the naturalized Indian Jean Drèze, whose concern is a state that is hostile and indifferent to its citizens, largely because it is busy running hotels and airlines and, therefore, lacks the capacity to intervene meaningfully in sanitation, public health or education. Drèze, despite being a hero of the left, makes a sound conservative case for building state capacity in the delivery of key public goods and in controlling corruption. What is forgotten is that the benefits of the actions of the Indian state go to the favoured rich. Examples abound. Fertilizer subsidies help fertilizer companies, not farmers. Free electricity helps rich farmers as poor farmers cannot afford pump sets. The poor, ostensibly on whose behalf these actions are undertaken, are in fact illusory beneficiaries at best.

Lal and Sen are moralists in the tradition of the Mahatma and Rajaji, fully acquainted with the ancient Indic attempt to square the circle while dealing with the creative tension between the pursuits of artha and dharma. The larger failure of the economics profession in India has been that it is stuck in trying to seek out a solution that works. In the process, we forget that Adam Smith supported markets not just because they work efficiently, but also because they pass the moral test of obtaining the approval of Smith's famous 'impartial spectator' – an imaginary being who represents our moral conscience.

We also ignore Tiruvalluvar's emphasis on the celebration of the sober pursuit of material wealth without interference from a tyrant, and Amartya Sen's concern for the development of capacities in human beings. The country, therefore, remains trapped in trying to do the minimum that it can get away with politically.

~

The founder of India's Planning Commission, Prasanta Mahalanobis was a leftist with an enduring affection for the Soviet Union. Mahalanobis and his friends left behind a legacy that has still not disappeared. Its residual influence is ongoing and strong. Being stuck in the groove of Mahalanobis and his friends, in believing that a single ideologically correct solution is possible, has resulted in a complete gridlock in environmental matters. Everything is adversarial. No compromises can be struck between mineral extraction and ecological concerns.

And adding another layer to this palimpsest is the fashionable urban concern for tribal populations who live within or on the peripheries of India's forests. The statist solution employed in the Soviet Union to the detriment of large waterbodies like the Aral Sea and the Caspian Sea is seen as the only alternative to Luddite non-development. The fact that several countries and societies within the world of relatively free markets have managed to balance matters and dramatically improve air and water quality is simply ignored.

More importantly, the moral arguments are presented only in extreme terms. 'Abandon all development and become hunter-gatherers' or 'set up roads, dams and mines indiscriminately, and it is perfectly all right if these actions are undertaken by state enterprises, just don't let private, sorry, neo-liberal initiative prosper' – no nuance, no attention to the ancient idea of Sukshma Dharma, which acknowledges how subtle these issues are and how excruciatingly painful it is to tread the appropriate path that allows a human being to dig the earth while respecting her as mother.

The solution is not to abandon digging. The ploughman was Tiruvalluvar's hero. The author of the Tirukkural would have added that it is shameful to abandon the search for a balanced solution merely because it is difficult. And the detail is important – the fact is that we can rein in the so-called rapacious capitalists; we cannot rein in state enterprises. The pollution record of state enterprises in order of magnitude is worse than the record of their private sector counterparts. And this is not unique to India: Soviet state enterprises were just terrible; Chinese state enterprises are in the same mould.

～

In any event, the situation within the economics discipline is modestly sanguine from the point of view of the Indian conservative. Despite an ongoing guerrilla campaign against neo-liberalism, the statist central planners are in retreat. One would feel a lot better if the argument was won not just on the empirical plane by debating what works, but also on the moral plane by discussing why it is important that the unique and time-tested human institution of markets be preserved, protected and enhanced in order to sustain humanity's tryst with its own finer aspects, which after all has to be the firm wish of any full-blooded conservative.

And lest anyone think that markets were invented in the West, especially when your economic history professors tell you about the bancas in Florence, the Rialto in Venice or the coffee houses in Amsterdam and London – do pay attention to our own petas, mandis, santeys, bazaars and chowks. So even from the perspective of conservatism, which attempts to preserve the best in our past, we are on firm ground.

2

The Political Sphere

Let us now turn to politics, that most contentious and complex of human interests.

The fundamental political dispute that defined the first half of the twentieth century in India had to do with the approach to the Raj. Many conservatives believed that with all its faults, on balance the Raj must be leveraged as a force for the good. They were concerned, in typical conservative fashion, that in the pursuit of freeing India, we as a people should not jettison the good that inhered in British rule. It is not uncommon to keep running into the view that we were in a sense lucky not to have been colonized by the Portuguese, the Spanish, the Dutch or even the French. The Indian encounter with the Anglo-Saxon has been seen as one that resulted in a refreshing outburst of creativity, which had constructive outcomes. In independent India, such approaches have been characterized as traitorous and as representing the views of toadies or compradors, as Marxists like to argue. This has resulted in Indian conservatism being reviled and its serious study being neglected.

But we cannot let something as important as modern Indian conservatism be defined in a shallow manner and be peremptorily dismissed. The fact remains that India's conservatives were all good patriots who loved their country, unlike the communists who in mid-1941 switched from opposing dirty British imperialism to supporting the glorious Allied war effort, and who again argued in 1962 that the Chinese were liberators and not invaders. Their fellow travellers, the Naxalites, have gone on to argue that the murderous Chairman Mao was and perhaps is everyone's chairman.

There was a star-studded and respectable school of thought which held the well-considered view that British rule was not only an inescapable fact but also provided a positive injection into the stream of Indian history. Rammohun Roy laid the foundation for this school of thought. He believed that India needed many years of British rule for its own good. While his was an empiricist approach to practical requirements and to the need to change several aspects of Indian society, Bankim

Chandra had a more ideological and cultural view of the nature of British rule. Admittedly, he made changes to his celebrated *Anandamath*, toning down its anti-British elements in order to get it past British censors. But there is no reason to believe he did not subscribe to the view that British rule was providential and was going to help a revival and a creative renaissance among Hindus. Broadly speaking, Swami Vivekananda too subscribed to this view.

Perhaps no one combined love of the country, genuine concern for the welfare of its inhabitants, balanced admiration for the liberalizing and liberating aspects of British rule along with a commitment to gradual increased and finally complete political freedom for India than the brilliant Gopal Krishna Gokhale. To this day Gokhale remains one of the brightest stars in the Indian conservative firmament.

~

We need to deal with the Ram Guha question – the difference between liberals and conservatives. Are Rammohun Roy, Dadabhai Naoroji and Gokhale not liberals? They were and are frequently referred to in that vein. I believe it is important to remember that on the issue of evolutionary process, they were clearly conservative and not liberal in their outlook. They did not look for a top-down adoption of an abstract principle as a solution to society's problems. They were exemplary gradualists and looked for simultaneous political, social and economic change, much of which was to be initiated on a bottom-up basis by persons and voluntary associations.

Why then are they hailed as liberals by so many? This may be the result of an ironic historical contingency. Well into the nineteenth century, the George III–Lord North type of Tories continued to exercise their baneful influence in Britain. As a result, even though Rammohun Roy went to England as a very conservative emissary of the impoverished Mughal emperor, he was feted not by the High Church party, but by nonconformists like the Unitarians. Willy-nilly, even conservative Indians ended up being seen as liberal fellow travellers. In the decades that followed, British Tories preferred Indian maharajas to scholars like Naoroji. It was only the Liberal Party which would nominate Naoroji for a parliamentary seat. Gokhale faced the same situation. His only interested audience in England was to be found among liberals. The parallel with George III and Lord North is striking. In the 1770s, George III and Lord North obdurately refused to deal with genuine and important American leaders like Washington, Jefferson, Hamilton, Madison and Adams and kept propping up some dubious so-called loyalists. In subsequent centuries, large sections of the British ruling class adopted a similar approach towards important rising Indian leaders. Indian political leaders with any gravitas acquired the penumbra of being liberal, principally because British conservatives were silly. This silliness persisted into the 1930s. If Churchill's diehard supporters had not sabotaged early dominion status for India in that decade, a united India, oddly enough, might till today have been a British dominion. They did not listen to Burke when he argued for dealing sensitively with the American colonists. They lost the thirteen colonies which went on to become the United States of America. They did not listen to Stanley Baldwin, who would have preferred to grant dominion status to India in the 1930s. They lost India entirely. The parallel between Churchill and George III is not an original insight of mine. Leopold Amery, one of Churchill's friends and ministers, has left a record of his views on that subject. In any event, the foolishness of some (not all) British conservatives resulted in Indian leaders aligning themselves first with the Liberal Party in Britain, and subsequently with the Labour socialists.

Others emerged as supporters of British rule for different material and intellectual reasons. Jyotiba Phule and later Ramaswamy Naicker praised British rule for having liberated the lower castes and were very concerned that when the British left, an oppressive upper-caste, Aryanized Brahmin–Bania ruling class would emerge. Their intellectual descendants today can very well continue with the argument that this has in fact happened.

The historian Rajmohan Gandhi has pointed out that the Dalit leader Anchas had gone one step further when, in as early as 1917, he had argued that the departure of the British and the launch of Home Rule, whether by Brahmins or non-Brahmins, would crush the Dalits. Every time we read of an atrocity committed against Dalits today, perhaps we should remember this, be less vituperative about British rule and acknowledge that the Raj did have a liberating touch for India's downtrodden. For reasons of their own, persons as distinct as Behram Malabari, Pandita Ramabai, Cornelia Sorabji and others were also supporters of prolonged British rule. They believed that it prevented the emergence of a ruling elite dominated by the upper castes.

~

It is important to remember that conservatism always tends to be accompanied by constructive activity. Jyotiba Phule worked with the conservative scholar R.G. Bhandarkar to promote education. Ramaswamy Naicker came up with a simplified marriage ritual partly in order to reduce the ruinous costs of traditional Indian weddings. C.P. Ramaswami Aiyar made a somewhat eccentric argument that the leaders of the Indian nationalist movement like Gandhi and Nehru were psychologically unbalanced (!) and that the preservation of the princely order would be helpful to India.

The princely order had some worthy defenders, who cannot be easily dismissed. Mirza Ismail and M.A. Sreenivasan, who had been prime ministers of states like Mysore, Jaipur, Hyderabad and Gwalior, felt that the continuation of monarchies, even with some changes, would help maintain a sense of coherence and continuity.

In recent times, historians like Meghnad Desai and Zareer Masani have taken the position that a step-by-step constitutional development started with the Regulating Act and Pitt's India Act in the late 1700s, when the British Parliament began applying its mind to the complex and complicated challenges involved in governing India. This process logically culminated in the India Independence Act of 1947. It is important to note that all these moves originated in Westminster. This school downplays the theory that the nationalist freedom movement somehow 'snatched' freedom from the British and argues that India and Indian society in fact leveraged British rule to engage in constructive change. The embrace of the English language, the creation of

Indian political unity and the adoption of English legal institutions are seen as evidence of this.

Syed Ahmad Khan supported the continuation of British rule because he was suspicious that its substitution with a democratic polity or a purely meritocratic administration would be inimical to Muslim interests, both for the community at large and in the context of their having been the erstwhile ruling class.

Even within the nationalist movement, where the end of British rule was considered both inevitable and desirable, several political figures preferred dominion status and a continued association with Britain rather than opting for complete independence, which was the official stance of the Indian National Congress after 1929.

Even within the Congress, not all positions were identical. Rajagopalachari opposed the Quit India movement during the Second World War as he felt that this would only help the Japanese who were potentially more sinister rulers than the British ever could or would be. While the Congress party officially opposed co-operation with the British during the war, the Hindu Mahasabha encouraged volunteers to join the armed forces because after several centuries of systematic disarmament, Indians were being given an opportunity to acquire skills in modern warfare and military administration. Ambedkar remained a member of the

Viceroy's Council through the war. He too, like Phule and Naicker, was worried that liberating impulses acquired by lower castes under British rule might get compromised by high-caste majority hegemony.

To dismiss this wide range of support that the Raj was able to garner as unpatriotic, traitorous and smacking of complicit toadyism is silly. Many were certainly collaborators. But they were so because they felt that such collaboration was in the best interests of their country and their people, not because they were bribed with thirty pieces of silver, which in any case most of them neither needed nor wanted. Far from being a sin, constructive collaboration represents an extremely virtuous and, need I add, a dharmic response to a ruler or rulers, who like all rulers have both worthy and unworthy tendencies.

~

Let us get back to the two founders of modern Indian political conservatism – Rammohun Roy and Bankim Chandra Chatterjee – because they represent key divergences right at its origins. From Rammohun Roy was derived what I would call, broadly speaking, a Burkean tradition of Indian conservatism, which was keen to combine the best of Indian and British conservative ideas in order to come up with something that would work for India. Providential or not, British rule was a fact. The introduction of British systems in our legal and political life was also a fact. Almost tautologically the argument was made that the very fact that the British had conquered India and not vice versa implied that at least in matters military and administrative, we had something, and perhaps much, to learn from the British. To learn the English language, at a minimum for instrumentalist purposes, to adopt some variant of the English common law, and, where appropriate, to study and imitate British commercial and government institutions – all of these seemed eminently desirable to Rammohun Roy and those who followed him. Being conservatives, they embraced the fact that pursuit of political change alone, without concomitant economic and social changes, would lead the country down a destructive Jacobin path. Nothing summarizes the Indian conservative love affair with English constitutionalism and its disdain for French radicalism better than the words of the illustrious Indologist and social reformer R.G. Bhandarkar in his famous 1895 speech: 'We should not adopt the procedure of the French Revolution, but imitate the mode of action of the English people, whose pupils we are. They have realized as great changes as the French Revolution sought to effect, but in a manner which connects them with the past history of the country.' This single statement can be considered the high-water mark of nineteenth- and early-twentieth-century Indian conservatism.

Rammohun Roy's associate Dwarkanath Tagore started the first managing agency firm, a peculiarly Indian institution, which combined British joint stock ventures with the added need for trust in a society marked by so many cleavages and discontinuities. Gokhale's commitment to the Servants of India Society demonstrated his conviction that unless and until Indians took the initiative in areas like education and social reform, political aspirations would remain overly ambitious and a tad foolish. The social reformer Mahadev Govind Ranade felt that demands for political change should be postponed until substantial social reform had been achieved. Ranade was echoing the renowned Telugu writer and reformer Viresalingam. Viresalingam had categorically asserted that without reforming our social and religious conditions, Indians could not enjoy the fruits of political independence.

~

Even after the eclipse of Gokhale's ideas, there remained within the Congress party several persons who favoured positive responses to British moves like the Montagu–Chelmsford reforms of the 1920s, which increased Indian participation in the government of the country, and the Government of India Act of 1935, which for all practical purposes transferred all matters other than defence, foreign affairs and central finances to the Indian leadership. The 1935 Act turned out to be particularly important. Within the limitations of this Act, Rajagopalachari and his team of ministers in Madras managed to rise to the challenge of transforming themselves from agitators to administrators.

Congress radicals like Jawaharlal Nehru, Subhas Chandra Bose and Jayaprakash Narayan opposed these moves as smacking of collaboration and as not standing up for the extreme socialist and anti-capitalist manifesto which they forced through at the Karachi Congress.

As it turns out, it is precisely the socialistic vocabulary of the Karachi Congress which led to the emergence of another school of conservatives, this time within the Congress. This wing was represented by Rajendra Prasad, Sardar Patel and K.M. Munshi, among others, who became an effective counter to the Congress socialists inside the broad tent. The conjurer's trick that got the radical opponents of dominion status, the cheerleaders of a socialist, possibly even a Soviet, republic to agree to gradual change was played at Independence. Thanks to V.P. Menon's sagacity, Patel's practicality, and possibly Mountbatten's charm, even the meteoric Pandit Nehru was persuaded that dominion status for a few years was perfectly in order. This ensured that the newly formed Constituent Assembly did not opt for creating Soviets or communes, despite the great admiration for the Soviet Union that was common among many influential leftists.

~

The providential master stroke was inducting Ambedkar as the chairman of the Constituent Assembly's drafting committee. Ambedkar opted for the old conservative ideals of gradualism and not giving up the good with the bad. Our Constitution ended up relying heavily on the Government of India Act of 1935. Many may not know about it, because the hyper-patriotic National Council of Educational Research and Training (NCERT) textbooks do not bother to tell us much about this Act. Arguably, it is one of the finest pieces of legislation to come out of Westminster. An enormous amount of time was invested in it by many British parliamentarians. One noteworthy example stands out. He was a young, talented Labour Member of Parliament called Clement Attlee. He distinguished himself more than a decade later by piloting the India Independence Bill through the British Parliament. Leveraging the 1935 Act so extensively can be considered a tribute to Rammohun Roy's vision of a century earlier. We gave ourselves a Westminster-style Constitution with an independent judiciary, with citizens being protected by judicial writs of habeas corpus, mandamus and certiorari, with a clear emphasis on civilian control of the military, and so much more. Luckily for us, despite Nehru's admiration for Lenin, when push came to shove, he went along with the ancient English Magna Carta traditions, which emphasized individual liberty and the rule of law and not with the ideas, if that's the appropriate word, of the Petrograd Soviet. Clearly, the conservative caucus managed to outsmart the noisy Congress socialists.

In the original Constitution, before its more recent unfortunate amendments, property was retained as a fundamental right. If the sovereign can take away an individual's property without due process and compensation, then all claims to liberty become meaningless. Burke knew this. Adam Smith emphasized this, and some two thousand years ago Tiruvalluvar stood up for this. In any event, the doctrines of gradual change and not throwing out the baby with the bathwater prevailed. India's was an evolutionary independence, not a revolutionary one. There is a warm feeling when we realize that for seven decades we have retained the same Constitution, albeit with amendments both desirable and not so good. Contrast this with Latin American countries, where constitutions are frequently abandoned and replaced with caricatures. Continuity, legislated change, following due process and ensuring the legitimacy of the republic – all these are the fine legacies we have become heirs to.

~

The economist and columnist Swaminathan Aiyar has pointed out to me that I am precipitating a degree of semantic confusion about what constitutes conservatism, which might render not just this section but the entire range of my arguments open to criticism. He is particularly concerned with describing the Indian Constitution as a conservative document. Given that in one stroke it prohibits discrimination on the basis of caste, gender or religion, all so deeply embedded in our history and our country, would it not be more appropriate to call it a revolutionary document, far from being a conservative one? Grappling with Aiyar's argument has forced me to pay greater attention to the historical process of how our Constitution evolved. It was not simply written up in one day or, for that matter, in three or four years. It is the culmination of a process of gradual change and in fact has far greater claim to conservative credentials than revolutionary ones.

Let's start with viewing the territory of India as a

political unit. This dates back to the Regulating Act of the late 1700s. Till this Act came into force, the governors of Madras, Bombay and Bengal each had a direct reporting relationship with the East India Company head office on Leadenhall Street in London. The Regulating Act decided to refer to the governor of Bengal as the governor general and had the two other governors reporting into Calcutta. This simple step began the political and administrative unification of India.

Just think of the counterfactual. If Madras and Bombay had continued as independent colonial entities, we might have seen the emergence of separate nation states, like what happened in French Indochina. It is interesting to note that Ceylon was always run separately and Calcutta and Simla had no say over that island's affairs. Indian Civil Service officers were never sent to Ceylon. Instead, the British officials there came from the Colonial Civil Service. The Colombo government reported to the Colonial Office in London and not to the India Office. If that had not been the case, Sri Lanka might today have been part of the contemporary Indian nation state. The case with Burma is interesting in that it was the other way around. Burma was run from Calcutta till 1937, when its administration was separated from India. And Myanmar today is clearly a separate country.

The point I wish to make is that the territorial

political unity blithely and casually assumed in our 1950 Constitution is in fact the result of two centuries of evolution. The proposal put forward by the British Viceroy Wavell in 1946 that Britain should withdraw province by province and hand over power to provinces would have resulted in undoing the effects of the Regulating Act, which had in fact brought the provinces, or presidencies as they were then called, under one rubric. Wavell's plan would have been revolutionary. Wavell's successor, Mountbatten, too toyed with this idea. Luckily, a clever V.P. Menon and a febrile Nehru torpedoed this plan. If Subhas Chandra Bose's Indian National Army (INA) had dominated free India, we would have had the possibility of a Prussian state replacing the Raj, and civilian control of the military might have been at risk. As it turns out, this did not happen. On balance, it was Partition that was an abrupt, radical and possibly revolutionary act, not the Indian Independence Bill on its own, or even the new Constitution of India.

~

One can argue that the idea of non-discrimination too had an evolutionary history through the Raj. The jury is out on whether the Manusmriti was simply an idealized text or if it was practised. But for what it is worth, it did have a measure of social sanction and it did provide for differential punishments for identical crimes committed by persons belonging to different castes. It turns out that the Raj successfully subverted this ideology fairly early in the game. By confirming the rather dubious and unfair hanging of the Brahmin Nuncomar, Justice Impey categorically established that caste status would not come in the way of state punishments. Nuncomar was hanged for the crime of forgery, which was not a capital crime in Hindu or in Mughal traditions. However, contemporary accounts would suggest that the Indian public in Calcutta was less concerned about this technicality and upset because Nuncomar was a high-born Brahmin!

Macaulay's Indian Penal Code was also clear that individuals would be tried and punished as individuals and not as members of a caste or religious group. Queen Victoria's Proclamation in 1858 went a step further and emphatically affirmed non-discrimination on racial, religious or caste lines. The fact that it was not always practised does not take away from its salience and importance.

Even in the area of gender, the practices of the Raj were not necessarily much behind those prevalent in Britain and America. In the late nineteenth century, the Madras Medical College did admit women. In the early twentieth century, Cornelia Sorabji was not allowed to practise in the Bombay High Court because women were not allowed to practise in English courts at that time. The enhancement of women's rights can also be seen as a gradual and phased affair, rather than one which was parachuted in by our Constitution.

Some have argued that the grant of universal adult franchise by our Constitution was truly revolutionary. While this may be a source of pride for some Indians, the fact of the matter is that franchise in the Government of India Act was restricted not on the basis of identities like caste, religion or gender, but on the basis of objective criteria like age, income, property ownership and education. It is important to remember that Dalits, who had no civic rights under the dispensation of the Manusmriti, were important voters in British India. In 1950, we merely altered the objective criteria, by sticking only to age. Our claim to fame may be that we tried very hard and substantially succeeded in practising what our Constitution preached. The denial of the vote to African Americans for a century after they obtained the legal right stands in stark contrast.

Incidentally, a similar argument can be made about the American Constitution, that it was a revolutionary and not a conservative document. It got rid of monarchy. After all, it was written post a so-called revolutionary war. The votaries of this argument forget that the thirteen colonies were in fact protesting the changes that George III and Lord North were trying to force on to colonies endowed with century-old charters. As Burke pointed out, the British were being anything but conservative in dealing with their North American colonies. The framers of the American Constitution were extremely particular about maintaining continuity with their inherited Anglo-Saxon political traditions. They were, like all good conservatives, aiming to preserve the best parts of their inheritance. This contrasted with the French revolutionaries who wanted to erase all traces of the ancien régime.

The very chronology by which the political institutions of India evolved from the Regulating Act, Pitt's India Act, the Charter Acts, Queen Victoria's Proclamation, the creation of Councils, the Minto–Morley Reforms, the Montagu–Chelmsford Act and the 1935 Government of India Act all the way to our Constitution makes it an evolutionary, gradual, constitutional process. The retention of the key features of the political institutions bequeathed to us by the Raj makes the process a conservative one. The new Constitution did go against doctrines like the Manusmriti. But that process had started long ago. There was no revolutionary abruptness to our Constitution. We did not have a war with our erstwhile rulers. This ensured the absence of sweeping change.

Partition was a different matter altogether. After

having had a single governor general for two and a half centuries, we suddenly got two – Mountbatten and Jinnah. This was sudden and anything but evolutionary. Despite its most prominent advocate, Jinnah, arguing that after Partition two brothers would live in peace, this 'revolutionary' act was accompanied by massive, insensate violence as is to be expected from such happenings. The real revolutionary was Jinnah, not Gandhi or Nehru or Ambedkar or Patel or Rajagopalachari. The inability of Pakistan to retain cohesion or to acquire constitutional continuity can be considered the inevitable gift of a revolution. It is perhaps time for Pakistani intellectuals to pause and reread Burke's *Reflections on the Revolution in France*.

While the Rammohun Roy tradition culminated in our Constitution, the Bankim tradition was not altogether absent. The fact that for Hindus, British rule meant a historic opportunity to recover from past defeats inevitably resulted in a Hindu revivalist movement coming into being. Given the amorphous nature of the phenomenon known as Hinduism, there were, by definition, numerous movements which originated in different parts of the country and the emphasis of each of them tended to be different. One thing, however, that was common was a certain sense of pride in the country's distant past. The common myth became that, for a variety of reasons, Hindus had lost out, degenerated and not lived up to the high standards set by their ancestors. Now was the time to recover ancient glory. Current Hindu weaknesses were not seen as intrinsically and originally Hindu, but as aberrant accretions that had arisen due to the exigencies of history. This view was shared by the Brahmo Samaj, the Ramakrishna Mission, the Prarthana Samaj, the Arya Samaj and even by movements like the Sree Narayan Dharma Paripalana Yogam, the Swaminarayan movement, the Theosophical Society and the Aurobindo Ashram. These institutions and movements were primarily religious, philosophical, theological and social. For politics, the Indian National Congress seemed to serve the needs of the Bankim school for three decades after 1885. Hindu revivalists like Malaviya, Lajpat Rai and Tilak were comfortable within the Congress.

As it turns out, similar, although not identical, developments were taking place among Indian Muslims and their leadership groups. Moderate Muslims like Badruddin Tyabji were comfortable with the Congress. Sir Syed Ahmad Khan opposed the Congress as he was suspicious of its inevitable Hindu majority. He also felt that it was preferable for Indian Muslims to eschew political activity altogether and focus on improving their educational status within the protective canopy of the Raj. The north Indian Muslim elite nevertheless panicked as they witnessed gradual political change initiated by the British, which they felt was detrimental to Muslim interests. Sir Syed was dead and his restraining influence was gone. With encouragement from several British officials and British academics attached to the Aligarh College, a group of upper-class north Indian Muslims formed the Muslim League in 1906. They were conservatives insofar as they were supporters of the Raj status quo. But in a loose sense of the term, they were also reactionaries. They looked back to a time when they believed that their direct ancestors ruled large parts of India. It was not accidental that many of the founders of the Indian Muslim League claimed to be descendants of nawabs.

～

The first exclusive national Hindu political organization separate and distinct from the Congress was the Hindu Mahasabha, which was set up in 1915, to some extent as a reaction to the establishment of the Muslim League. The Hindu Mahasabha felt that the Congress exhibited a great eagerness to be Indian in a non-partisan way. This resulted in the Congress betraying Hindu interests. Oddly enough, this remains a significant issue to this day.

One of the concerns of Hindu nationalists is that in its attempt at even-handedness, the Indian state does not treat its Hindu majority with the respect it deserves. While the Hindu nationalist movement gradually diverged from the Congress, for many years it was not unusual for a Hindu leader to be a member of the Congress and the Hindu Mahasabha simultaneously, just as it was not unusual for a Muslim leader to be a member of the Congress and the Muslim League.

The Hindu nationalist movement was itself reasonably polychromatic. Senior leaders like Madan Mohan Malaviya and Hans Raj Gupta were not vehemently ill-disposed to British rule and believed that focus on education by the Hindus was an important prerequisite for meaningful political reform. They even advocated English education. Moonje and Savarkar derived their intellectual inspiration from the more militant and radical traditions of Tilak. Their support for some aspects of the Raj tended to be instrumental. If tactical cooperation with the Raj could help Hindus, then they were all for it. The observations of the writer and parliamentarian Swapan Dasgupta make it clear that the custom of viewing the Raj instrumentally goes all the way back to the traditionalist school led by Radhakanta Deb. The big worry of the traditionalist school was that the denouement resulting from an early British withdrawal, before a strong Hindu revival and consolidation was in place, would not be a good one.

Moonje and Savarkar were also concerned that an excessive focus on Gandhian non-violence might leave the Hindus weak as a collective and susceptible to foreign domination again. In this respect, they echoed Bankim considerably.

In 1925, Hedgewar and his lieutenant Golwalkar left the Hindu Mahasabha to form the RSS, which they positioned as a social and cultural organization. They believed that unless family and neighbourhood Hindu organizations were strengthened, any political superstructure created would be weak. They also emphasized charitra, or character, and character-building among their members. The echoes from the historian Jadunath Sarkar, who considered character a key element in the unfolding of national destiny, are obvious here.

The Hindu nationalist movement was strong in northern, central and western India, with a Bengali layer added to it. The south, with its Aryan–Dravidian and Brahmin–non-Brahmin identity issues, remained at best peripheral to the efforts to mobilize people and energies around a Hindu cause.

Both the Hindu Mahasabha and the RSS got their leadership from the upper castes. But both were resolute and loud in their rejection of caste as detrimental to the evolution of a consolidated Hindu nationalism. Of course, in this regard they were no different from the Congress or the communists, both dominated by upper castes, and the Muslim League, where leadership was in the hands of the Ashraf elite.

The question that arises is whether the pre-Independence Hindu nationalist movement was a conservative one or not. It certainly had a conservative flavour to it, but it also had a revivalist and rejectionist flavour. It viewed the British association as primarily of instrumental value. It had a sceptical view of English education, which could weaken the cultural moorings of Hindus, who did not seem to have an identity strong enough to resist the material and intellectual seduction that English education almost inevitably entailed. This was particularly so when contrasted with Muslims, who were able to defend their identity by virtue of it being grounded in strong common religious beliefs. The ongoing creative tensions between the Fukuzawa school, which sought a benign Japanese modernization, and the Samurai–Mishima school, which believed in the kind of aggressive cultural assertion that characterizes Japanese politics, had very similar trends within the Hindu nationalist movement.

My friend the polychromatic scholar and technocrat Kiran Karnik has argued with me that 'Hindu conservatism' as a descriptor may be better received by commentators and critics than the expression 'Hindu nationalism'. There is something here that appeals to the bourgeois sensibility. Hindu conservatives can be seen as intellectually and politically akin to European Christian Democrats, and the 'fascist taint' associated with the expression 'nationalism' can be avoided. Unfortunately, words and expressions acquire meanings within historical and geographical contexts. When one thinks of the expression 'Hindu conservatism', the images that come to mind are of obscurantism, support of caste, sati, purdah, dowry and other such practices. It goes against the grain of Disraeli's dictum of abandoning the weaknesses of the past, and of Burke's position that we must change in order to conserve.

The expression 'Hindu nationalism' may raise the shackles of leftists. But that's hardly a reason to oppose it. I might even add, only in a partially tongue-in-cheek manner, that such opposition might be a good reason to support Hindu nationalism, which at least does attempt to create an associative 'band of brothers' across castes and regions. It does not defend the more baneful aspects of our inheritance. That it does not extend the concept of 'band of brothers' beyond the Hindu grouping may be because we have gone along with British census officials in embracing a religious definition of the word 'Hindu'. If we made it cultural and altered Hindu to Indic, would that satisfy the critics? Then it is easily done. But that will not end the debate. Syed Ahmad Khan and Iqbal would, from their perspectives, assert the importance of religious identity. Marxists, Freudians and postmodernists reject the existence of an overarching culture, irrespective of whether you call it India, Indic or Hindu. It is obviously so much easier to be a Japanese than an Indian. Both our cultures would agree that this is precisely the nature of karmic destiny, which cannot be altered by choosing different words or expressions. So Hindu nationalism it is. And the argument as to whether it is a subset of Indian conservatism or merely another school with some overlaps will continue till the cows come home, or in this case, till the holy cows come home.

~

In the limited franchise elections under the 1935 Act, the Hindu Mahasabha had some success, even as the Congress emerged as the dominant political party of the Hindu electorate. It is important to remember that both in Sind and in Bengal, the Hindu Mahasabha and the Muslim League cooperated in coalition governments. This astonishing detail, which pretty much weakens the argument made by many critics to this day that the Hindu nationalist movement had an inherent anti-Muslim strain to it, is rarely given publicity. To the contrary, the Hindu nationalist movement repeatedly demonstrated a practical empiricism, worthy of the best conservatives. And this was done despite the relatively strong positions of persons like Savarkar and Golwalkar who had an inherent suspicion about Muslim loyalties. The fact that Muslim League leaders may not have thought of India as a holy land did not mean that in the interests of pragmatic progress, Hindu Mahasabha leaders would not consent to be junior members of coalition governments where the League was the dominant partner. Even as his fellow Bengali Subhas Bose was supporting a Japanese invasion of India, the Hindu Mahasabha leader Shyamaprasad Mukherjee was absolutely clear that the Japanese must be resisted and his party supported Indian recruitment into the Raj's armed forces in order to ensure this was the case. The contrast with the equivocating position of the Congress leaders who both supported and opposed Bose could not be clearer.

This clarity on the part of the Hindu Mahasabha should also put to rest the oft-repeated argument that this organization was pro-fascist. It was Bose who was pro-fascist, not Mukherjee. And let us not forget Bose won the Congress presidency fair and square at Haripura and Tripuri. One wonders if this could have formed the basis of the contention that the majority of Congress members of that time were pro-Hitler and pro-Tojo. As an aside, one should note that Bose who was twice officially elected as the president of the Congress tried hard to enter Stalin's Soviet Union. Of course, there is no dearth of evidence that many in the Congress were admirers of that murderous Georgian apparatchik.

It is true that several Hindu nationalist ideologues were attracted to racist doctrines. One forgets that in the 1920s and 1930s, persons as diverse as Bernard Shaw, Margaret Sanger and Marie Stopes, not to mention the democratic government of the US, were ardent believers in eugenics. Genetic science had not progressed at that time to posit the existence of a common mitochondrial African mother for all humans. To keep on accusing Hindu nationalists of racism based on these dated writings is a little bit like judging Mahatma Gandhi as a racist because some researchers have discovered random statements from his South African period, where he was not sufficiently pro-black or was insensitive by today's standards of political correctness.

Having said all of this, there remains an ongoing tension between conservatism proper and revivalism. Both are concerned about not jettisoning the past. Revivalists, however, are focused on the distant past and tend to discount the immediate past. Conservatives attach equal importance to all periods of the past. In India, Hindu revivalists have emphasized the distant past and been negative about British rule, particularly seeing it as culturally debilitating, hence the accusation that English education leads to the creation of rootless Macaulay-putras. Conventional conservatives would take the position that British rule too is a valid part of our history and even though Macaulay was pompous and vain, the fact of the matter is that English is now part of the fabric of India. Jettisoning English would be a distinctly non-conservative act. In practical terms, this makes little sense. It will weaken India economically and needlessly alienate the southern states. Some of these issues are significant while others are in the nature of nuances. They keep recurring as examples where Hindu nationalists depart from mainstream conservatives.

In the 1946 elections, the Hindu Mahasabha was pretty much wiped out. The Congress emerged virtually as the sole representative of the Hindus of India, and despite the Congress's pretensions to the contrary, it was rejected by the limited franchise Muslim voters in India. Barring Bengal, Assam and Sind, the Congress lost virtually all the Muslim seats in the United Provinces, the Central Provinces, Orissa, Madras and Bombay. The exception of the North-West Frontier Province (NWFP) remains to this day a poignant one. With the Congress being the undisputed Hindu party, the raison d'être for the existence of the Hindu Mahasabha seemed to have disappeared. Independence and Partition brought many changes, which we will presently discuss.

~

For south Indians, the central theme of the twentieth century was the departure of the British who dominated the peninsula for two centuries after the battle of San Thome in 1740 and the fall of Seringapatam in 1799, and who then suddenly packed up and left, leaving us to deal with our language and caste issues pretty much on our own, with a north Indian elder brother breathing down our necks. For north Indians, for some reason, the haunting central theme has been not so much the British departure, but the Partition of India. There are hundreds of books, tracts and essays on the subject of Partition and on whether it could have been avoided. Conservatives felt, and rightly so, that the political and administrative unification of India was a reasonably precious matter. Throwing this away abruptly, especially with its attendant violence that bordered on a civil war, was tragic.

The principal issue, as it turned out, did not lie with revivalist Muslims like the Deobandis. It was the Muslim elites who found the idea of democratic franchise problematic. The British had accommodated them with the sinister and dangerous gift of separate electorates. In one stroke, the ability to create bonds of nationhood by positing a horizontal 'band of brothers' disappeared. The Mahatma had prophetically perceived this when the British Prime Minister Ramsay MacDonald had tried to offer separate electorates to the Dalits. If that had gone through, an Indian nation would have been a complete non-starter. The Mahatma went on a fast unto death opposing that diabolical move. Separate Muslim electorates unfortunately pre-dated Gandhi's entry into Indian politics.

The conservative elements in the Congress offered the Muslim elites a variant of the American model where people of different faiths could inhabit a common territory, with common laws and ideals. Given that culture has been more important for us than laws or ideals, this approach always had a limited chance of success. The historian Ayesha Jalal, among others, has emphasized how important the idea of an Indian Muslim culture was to so many leaders and their followers.

The radical elements in the Congress, represented by Nehru and Bose, simply pretended that the concerns of the Muslim elites were irrelevant: if class, and not caste or faith, was the only materially relevant reality, and if religion was the opium of the people, the Muslim League leaders, like opium addicts, had to be ignored. The leaders of the Muslim League disregarded both the conservative and radical sections of the Congress and their offers. Gandhi offered a third alternative that emphasized a soft, brotherly love. Despite sounding impractical, woolly-headed and surreal, this approach might just have worked, as it did for a few years in the 1920s. But the trust between the two by now distinct bands of brothers was missing.

If there had been joint electorates, so central for developing Scruton's shared mutuality between people living in the same neighbourhood, then it is quite likely that between 1909 and 1947, a common sense of nationhood would have developed. This reminds us of the contingencies of history. But that possibility had long disappeared. Muslim leaders over time were cornered into taking more extreme positions.

They received ideological comfort from persons like Muhammad Iqbal, who emerged as a sort of Islamic faux Nietzsche. Iqbal's ideas fell on fertile ground because from Sheikh Sirhindi's times, going back five hundred years, there had always been a school which disdained accommodation with the large number of Hindu, or more appropriately speaking, non-Muslim people living in the land, as the expression 'Hindu' hardly existed in Sirhindi's times. The Hindu nationalists argued that Indian Muslims should accept they were largely converts and were culturally Hindus. Nehru's Congress followers wanted poor Indian Muslims to disown their richer Ashraf brethren. The rest of the Congress and the Mahatma seemed to be offering only anodyne words. And let us not forget the British. People like the diplomat and historian Narendra Singh Sarila have made the case that Partition was driven in large measure by the sober calculations of British politicians and generals that Pakistan would be a Western ally, something that free India would never agree to. The delightful character Sir Humphrey Appleby from the *Yes Minister* books and TV series has reminded us that partition was British policy in Ireland, Palestine and India.

If Baldwin's views had prevailed and had not been stymied by Churchill and his diehard supporters, an interesting conservative option would have been to go for dominion status as early as 1935 and perhaps inducting the Prince of Wales as the constitutional head of an undivided India. If Hindu and Muslim sepoys in 1857 had respected the titular Mughal emperor, one wonders if this might not have worked. Critics will scoff that this is a wholly fanciful idea. But history is about contingencies. If George III and Lord North had listened to Burke, the Anglo-American relationship might have evolved quite differently. Anyway, let us not bother ourselves too much with counterfactuals. History moves on past both sunlit and sunless doorways.

~

Partition disrupted the gradual development of the Indian polity from the days of the Regulating Act and Pitt's India Act down to the Government of India Act of 1935. Partition was very costly in economic terms, as so much of our trade and transportation links were along the east–west axis. Partition increased the defence costs of both countries and has probably been ruinous for Pakistan. Above all, the human cost of Partition has been incalculable. The number of killed, raped, mutilated and displaced continues to breed despair and guilt in our hearts. Conservatives know that the bitter consequences of violent change last for decades and sometimes centuries. We are living with them. But we have to be realistic empiricists. We have to move on. After all, following Cornwallis's surrender at Yorktown, which brought an end to the American War of Independence, two prosperous English-speaking nations emerged in North America. While the US became an independent republic, Canada remained within the British Empire and subsequently within the British Commonwealth. Singapore has become a great city state, perhaps precisely because it broke off from the Malayan peninsula. And Bangladesh, which when it split from Pakistan was heralded by the omniscient Kissinger as a basket case, is doing quite well, thank you, both in human development indicators and in terms of economic growth rates.

The first conservative axiom is to wish our neighbours well. In this we adopt Tiruvalluvar and not Kautilya. Adam Smith and Hume repeatedly warned that both Britain and France would suffer if they envied each other. Unfortunately, no one listened to them. Sardar Patel captured this well when he said that 1947 was an opportunity for the Congress and the Muslim League to develop both their countries. Ever the empiricist, he felt that the alternative of two groups tugging in different directions was impractical. Rajagopalachari was always clear that we had a vested interest in Pakistan's success. Even Nehru was pretty clear that Partition was a fact and both countries had to hack it, however well or badly they thought fit. India has had a history of invasions from Afghanistan and Persia. We should welcome the existence of a buffer state of Pakistan between India and potential intruders. It should be our wish that the buffer remain and not disintegrate.

Conservatives need to oppose two important strands in Indian political thinking. The first is the view that India's relative success and Pakistan's relative failure will in some complicated manner prove that secularism is superior to theocracy. This is a dubious argument as it fails to take into account the myriad contingencies involved in history's cunning corridors and by-lanes. Whatever constitutional choices we wish to stay with, let them be derived from first principles and let them stand on their own and not depend on someone else's misfortune.

The second view, which is even more dangerous, is that we should try to reverse Partition and somehow become one happy family all over again. What well-meaning but clearly dim-witted Indians do not realize is that statements like these instil mortal fear in the Pakistani ruling elites. It has now become gospel truth among many of them that we want to conquer them and reincorporate them into our country. This causes them to go in for irrational actions, in order to deal with a non-existent threat being conveyed to them by the lovers of reversing history who are otherwise busy lighting goodwill candles.

Partition has happened. We wish each other well and move on. Incidentally, it took a hard-headed Hindu nationalist to understand the importance of words and gestures, something no left-wing sentimentalist would have understood or appreciated. Vajpayee visited the Pakistan Monument in Lahore and reassured Pakistanis that we accepted their national existence with no reserve. As for some intractable issues like Kashmir, cross-border terrorism and nuclear tension, they have each to be tackled separately, quietly and with the profound insight that no happy or permanent solution might emerge for long years to come.

~

For the first three years of Independence till the new Constitution came into force, the Rammohun Roy tradition of conservatism held sway in the country. The erudite conservative Rajendra Prasad presided over the Constituent Assembly. The incandescent conservative Rajagopalachari succeeded Mountbatten as the governor general. Ambedkar, a former member of the Viceroy's Council, became the chairman of the drafting committee for the Constitution. Sardar Patel did defang the princely order, not a very conservative thing to do, but he understood the value of continuity, even if only symbolic. He created rajpramukhs galore. The finest conjuring tricks were to proclaim the obdurate Nizam as Rajpramukh of Hyderabad and the prickly Maharaja of Udaipur as the Maharajpramukh of Rajasthan.

Patel also insisted on the abolition of separate electorates, which as all conservatives know is detrimental to shared mutuality, which is central to the conservative vision of communities and countries. What many do not know was that Patel presided over the committee that enshrined freedom of religion and the freedom to propagate religious views in the Constitution.

The original Constitution that was adopted in 1950, before recent mendacious amendments, consciously chose not to use the word 'secular'. It did open with the words 'We the people of India'. Given the recent Partition of India and the more recent incorporation of princely states, it is fatuous to argue that persons as sharp and eminent as Prasad, Patel, Ambedkar, Alladi Krishnaswami, K.M. Munshi and Nehru simply thought of India as a territorial state. I would argue that 'we the people' is meant to be a reference to people with a shared culture, however limited or tenuous that idea may be. We call it Indian culture. The fact that many of its traditional elements have a Hindu touch does not make it an exclusively Hindu culture. The Ramayana and the Mahabharata are doubtless central. But so are the Jataka tales, Jain sutras, Sufi music, the Sikh gurbani, Reverend Beschi's Tamil epic *Thembavani*, Abraham Panditar's Carnatic music compositions on Jesus, Avestan verses, Bene Israel psalms, Santhal chants and so much more. It seems glaringly obvious that 'we the people', at least for us, is not based solely or simply on territory or even on ideas, but on an extraordinarily imagined idea of India, which has been ours through 'trackless centuries' – and here I use an expression of Pandit Nehru's.

To make my conservative case even stronger and more universal, let me suggest that when the American founding fathers used the same evocative phrase 'we the people' they did not just refer to the inhabitants of thirteen colonies. They referred to the descendants of persons who had sought religious freedom, political liberty and economic opportunity in the New World, but who saw themselves very much as inheritors of the Magna Carta and its related Anglo-Saxon political culture, whose best elements were to be preserved. Subsequent immigration cannot change this historical fact. The Indian Constitution that emerged ends up in the same category, even as it sticks firmly to a conservative line, preserving the best elements of the Anglo-Saxon Raj.

In the early years after 1947, the conservative elements in the cabinet were able to recruit that arch-anti-conservative Jawaharlal Nehru to their side in the determined effort to crush a communist insurrection in south-central India. After 1950, the Indian political conservative cause was in trouble. Patel died. Ambedkar left the cabinet. Rajagopalachari withdrew to deal with the communists in Madras. Rajendra Prasad took up a ceremonial post. Within the Congress party, Purushottam

Das Tandon, who represented the Hindu revivalist caucus, was elbowed out. Nehru, an acolyte of the Fabians and an admirer of the Soviet Union, gradually became more and more powerful. Given the overwhelming political strength of the Congress party, conservatives had no choice but to operate through friendly caucuses within the Congress. The political scientist Rajni Kothari has brilliantly analysed how caucuses operate in a one-party-dominant democracy.

Given Nehru's strength, conservatives found the task of influencing the Congress from the outside an uphill one.

On foreign and defence policy matters, Nehru placed excessive reliance on the pro-communist Krishna Menon. This resulted in considerable damage to relations with Western democracies and a considerable cosying up with the Soviet Union and Communist China.

On economic issues, the statistician Mahalanobis emerged as an important adviser to Nehru. Mahalanobis seems to have believed that a somewhat mechanistic input–output model governed the economy, and he was convinced that central planning could ensure that the input–output model was controlled. In this world view, very little attention was paid to price signals, markets or incentives faced by economic actors. Mahalanobis had a penchant for inviting so-called foreign economic experts to visit India for a few weeks or months at a time, and then proceeding to give ex cathedra advice. It was orientalism all over again, but now without even the rooted knowledge and experience of Indian Civil Service officers. Names like Nicholas Kaldor, Roy Harrod and Evsey Domar, all committed to varying degrees of Keynesian state intervention, come to mind. The irony is that the free market guru Milton Friedman was invited and his advice was ignored. The transition from Mahalanobis's disastrous Gosplan documents to catastrophic fiscal, monetary and so-called industrial policies on the ground was accomplished by another Nehru acolyte, T.T. Krishnamachari, who joined the Congress after Independence and made an excellent career for himself. Krishnamachari appears to have been keen to prove himself more socialist than his leader, the well-meaning Pandit Nehru.

The conservative caucus had to tread carefully. The caucus included Rajagopalachari, now in semi-retirement; Morarji Desai, the eccentric and rugged individualist from Bombay; G.B. Pant from Uttar Pradesh; and the irrepressible B.C. Roy from West Bengal. Between them, they tried their best to save the Indian economy from the excesses of Mahalanobis and Krishnamachari.

Despite the warning signals given by persons like the economist B.R. Shenoy, Friedman, Rajagopalachari and the socialist turned free marketer Minoo Masani, the state followed policies that ensured decades of low growth and continued poverty in an already poor country, as the government of India pursued needless plans involving state gigantism, hostility towards the private sector, discouragement of foreign private capital and a strangulation of entrepreneurship.

Gentle voices from the sidelines, of persons like Mirza Ismail, that large dams make very little economic sense, were brushed aside. Today it is fashionable for shrill activists to criticize large dams. We should not forget that conservatives were way ahead of their times in their opposition to Stalinist follies. Ram Guha has drawn my attention to a speech of Nehru's in 1958, which supported Sir Mirza's position. Unfortunately, that speech can only be seen as representing a lost opportunity to avoid the blunders of gigantism.

We must remember that once momentum is lost, recovery can take decades. Between 1945 and now, India's share in world trade has dropped by more than 50 per cent. Any businessperson will tell you that loss of market share on such a scale is very difficult to reverse. We had a thriving textile industry, which we hounded and persecuted. If we had planned consciously and deliberately for failure, we could not have done a better job.

Fortunately, Nehru did not adopt wholesale socialism.

For this, Indian conservatives should take some credit. For preventing Nehru from pursuing collective farming, we have to thank the Swatantra Party and Charan Singh who opposed collectivization tooth and nail. Fortunately, the end result was that the commissars of the Indian state did not pursue or kill the kulak equivalents of our country and we were spared the horrors of Stalinist and Maoist famines. Although Nehru opposed the Supreme Court's defence of the fundamental right to property, especially the provisions for fair and justiciable compensation when property was being acquired, he had the good sense to realize that trying to remove the right to property from the list of fundamental rights could backfire. That obscenity was visited upon us much later.

~

By the late 1950s, it was obvious that the conservative caucus within the Congress was becoming ineffective as far as economic policies were concerned. This is when a bunch of brilliant patriotic intellectuals formed the Swatantra Party, which to this day remains a shining pole star in the Indian conservative sky. Rajagopalachari, Minoo Masani, N.G. Ranga, the Raja of Ramgarh, N. Dandekar, M. Ruthnaswamy, Piloo Mody, Viren Shah and H.M. Patel were joined by the Orissa leader

R.N. Singh Deo and the charismatic Maharani Gayatri Devi of Jaipur in this endeavour. The Swatantra Party opposed the invidious permit licence raj, which suited the growing public sector bureaucracies and many time-serving crony capitalists. The Swatantra Party gained traction in the 1962 elections even when Nehru was alive.

With Nehru's passing, there was a very real chance that, prodded from the outside by the Swatantra Party, the conservatives and pragmatists within the Congress would assert themselves. The early death of Lal Bahadur Shastri hurt this sanguine prospect. Indira Gandhi started off with a mixed ideological bag. She had demonstrated resolute anti-communism in 1959. She started her prime ministerial role with an imaginative devaluation of the rupee. But not being very conversant with economics, she failed to appreciate the importance of other necessary measures, including the elimination of industrial licensing. Seeing that her partial flirtation with market-friendly measures had not paid her political dividends, she abruptly turned left. She listened to a cabal of communist fellow travellers she surrounded herself with, and every few months she came up with yet another legislation which strangled the economy.

Swaminathan Aiyar has made the case that some of Indira Gandhi's policies were driven by realpolitik. Princes supported the Swatantra Party. Therefore, their privy purses and privileges were abolished, setting the now familiar Indian precedent of reneging on solemn commitments, covenants and promises. Businesspersons were sympathetic to the Swatantra Party. So tie them up with MRTP, FERA and a dozen other acronyms and they shall dare not whimper, let alone bark. Foreign companies were more difficult to bully. So emasculate and even eliminate them, sector by sector. Start a new public sector company every week so their bureaucracies and their contractors become beholden to the state and to the ruling party. Whether they were sincere believers in socialism or used socialism as a fig leaf, the purveyors of these policies have the unique distinction of ensuring planned poverty in our fair land.

The Swatantra Party fought a noble rearguard battle. A combination of misplaced alliances and tactical mistakes set the party back. But what really caused its demise was the nature of electoral democracy itself. For a political party to survive in a large democracy, a market-oriented economic ideology is insufficient. It needs to develop a rainbow coalition, which usually favours redistribution of wealth through government intervention. Otherwise, it needs a hard-core social and cultural identity foundation, usually provided by race, religion, language or ethnicity, and in India by caste. Because the Swatantra Party opposed an interventionist state while simultaneously lacking an identity marker, the brilliance of its intellectual founders proved to be of little use. Years after its demise, the Swatantra Party received a backhanded compliment as some of its economic policies were at least adopted in part by Narasimha Rao. With the disappearance of the Swatantra Party, Indian politics has seen the lack of a convincing Burkean conservative group in the Rammohun Roy tradition.

～

Let us consider some other areas where Indian conservatives had both successes and failures in influencing the state in our one-party-dominant democracy. Language remained for many years a bitter and divisive issue. Conservatives like Rajagopalachari, who had left the Congress, found allies in C. Subramanian, Chintaman Deshmukh and M.C. Chagla within that party. Once more the benefits of gradual, evolutionary, constitutional change without jettisoning the baby with the bathwater came to India's rescue. Linguistic states were created, Hindi was supported, but most importantly, English was retained. Orientalists in London, Paris and New York, who had predicted the division of India on linguistic grounds, were proved wrong. The republic survived, even as neighbouring Pakistan and Ceylon became victims of self-inflicted wounds while they pursued radical language policies in favour of Urdu and Sinhala. It is an irony of history that the pompous, priggish, anti-conservative Whig Macaulay gave us the gift of the English language, of which we as conservatives have become lovers and defenders.

Early on in the game, Sardar Patel took pains to give clear signals that civilian control of the armed forces was not negotiable. His conversation with General J.N. Chaudhuri before Operation Polo in Hyderabad, which Chaudhuri headed, is reminiscent of Lincoln or Truman. Chaudhuri was assured of operational autonomy and support. But the key political decisions would remain with the political executive, where they rightfully belonged. The Rajni Kothari strategy of trying to influence caucuses inside the dominant party was used not only by conservatives, but also by our pro-Soviet, pro-Chinese Marxist friends.

Krishna Menon, who unfortunately had Nehru's strong support, took a different tack from Patel's. He opposed the army brass because he saw them as inheritors of the traditions of the army of the Raj, and therefore pro-Western in their outlook. He encouraged officers to bypass official channels and supported controversial time-servers like General B.M. Kaul, who owed his promotions to his political connections, and the naval officer

K.M. Nanavati, who got special treatment apropos of his crime because he was close to Nehru and Menon. The situation got so bad that the then army chief General Thimayya could have pulled off a coup if he had wished to. India was very fortunate that Thimayya was sensible and sacrificed his own career, instead of opting for the methods employed by Oliver Cromwell in England some four hundred years ago, when he used the army to bypass parliament. Such a development would have been disastrous. Ironically, the 1962 defeat at the hands of the Chinese, and the poor showing of General Kaul in that campaign, put paid to Kaul's own plans to stage a coup. Perhaps India's gods were behind our providential, if humiliating, defeat as they were sure that a coup by Kaul would have been catastrophic for our country.

~

Conservatives also failed to influence the Indian state's tribal policies. The sociologist Ghurye was ignored; the imaginative anthropologist Verrier Elwin was acknowledged half-heartedly. Ghurye favoured rapid integration of the tribals with the rest of Indian society. Elwin preferred a gradual and gentle approach. In retrospect, it is obvious that the ideas of both Ghurye and Elwin had plus points as well as drawbacks. What cannot be disputed is that the quaint idea that tribals had no agency of their own and that they needed to be protected by self-appointed commissars and tsars from that noble human institution, the market, smacks of orientalism and a Margaret Mead variety of anthropology, where tribals are viewed as helpless objects and not as active agents. Peoples and communities cannot be put into purdah that easily. The Indian state could have focused on building capacities among tribals for their encounter with markets and modern technology. Despite or because of Elwin's quasi-romantic love for tribals, the Elwin strategy did involve an attempt at capacity building, and it was not without success in places like Arunachal Pradesh. In other parts of the country, the pompous, clumsy Indian state was always on the ascendant. The Indian government deliberately sidelined conservative and traditional tribal leaders like Jaipal Singh in Jharkhand and the popular Pravir Chandra Bhanj Deo, the Raja of Bastar, who could have, and who probably would have, shepherded the people through gradual, constitutional and constructive change.

Bereft of credible interlocutors, the Indian state is left trying to use a heavy-handed bureaucratic apparatus to deal with alienated tribals. Tragically, in some parts of the country, tribals have come under the influence of Marxism. They are almost certainly unaware that Stalin and Mao indulged in the most genocidal practices against indigenous peoples who had the misfortune to face their wrath.

~

The Bankim tradition has followed a more chequered and sinusoidal course. The assassination of Mahatma Gandhi in January 1948 was a national tragedy. It also turned out to be a serious setback for Hindu nationalists. The assassin Nathuram Godse had left both the Hindu Mahasabha and the RSS in 1946. But this fact did not alter perceptions. Godse was seen as a fellow traveller and the militant undertones in Hindu nationalist ideology were substantially, and perhaps even comprehensively, discredited. The Hindu Mahasabha pretty much lost its relevance in the early 1950s, when Shyamaprasad Mukherjee quit and formed the Bharatiya Jana Sangh as a new political outfit. This party maintained a connection with the RSS from where it drew much of its leadership. The early death of Shyamaprasad hurt the party considerably in Bengal and it got transformed primarily into a north Indian regional party. The new generation of brilliant Bengali Hindu conservatives like Swapan Dasgupta provided a measure of intellectual heft to Hindu nationalism. But they essentially lost their native political constituencies and had to remain content as expatriate probashis. The Jana Sangh's strong opposition to the retention of English and its support for Hindi ensured that it faced great difficulty in gaining traction in non-Hindi states.

Hindu nationalists were forced to follow the Rajni Kothari strategy of trying to influence the dominant Congress party from without and within. This strategy had some success when K.M. Munshi, Sardar Patel and Rajendra Prasad were persuaded to support the reconstruction of the Somnath temple. But the strategy was not without its problems. Groups like the Ram Rajya Parishad painted themselves into an obscurantist corner by opposing changes in colonial Hindu legal codes. They got through to President Rajendra Prasad. But even that proved unsuccessful and pointless.

A more fundamental question systematically haunted the Hindu nationalist movement. In a free India, was there any need for a focus on Hindu revivalism and a restoration of Hindu pride? There was no longer a pressing threat of the British smothering Hindus. For all practical purposes, it now appeared that identity issues would coalesce around languages and possibly castes. Partition had removed the possibility of a revived Muslim domination.

A new intellectual contribution was made by Deendayal Upadhyaya, who articulated an ideology which attempted to be distinct and opposed to the Western binaries of capitalism and communism. His ideology relied on Indian traditions and advocated what he referred to as integral humanism. This can certainly be considered an important development which relied on foundations laid by Hindu thinkers like Swami Vivekananda and Aurobindo. It is interesting that the word 'Hindu' was missing from the expression 'Integral Humanism'. Political Hinduism seemed to be bypassing its Hindu element. It was as though Hindu nationalism was pretty much on the sell list or even the short-sell list of astrologers, who were predicting its early demise. But as they say, political history is a minefield for all soothsayers. Unlike the fate of the Swatantra Party, the intellectual and political descendants of the Jana Sangh were to go from strength to strength. And that is another story, which will bring us to contemporary times.

~

The RSS acquired a fresh lease of life during Indira Gandhi's ill-fated Emergency, when it emerged as one of the few credible centres of resistance. This benefited the Jana Sangh, when it entered the Janata Party in 1977 as a respected entity. With the break-up of the Janata Party, the Jana Sangh converted itself into the

Bharatiya Janata Party (BJP). This new entity at first tried to understate Hindu nationalism and opt for something called Gandhian socialism. Very soon, it came to the conclusion that such expressions confused its supporters. This is not dissimilar to lessons learnt by the Republican Party in the US, whose compassionate capitalism made them similar to the Democrats, and the Labour Party in Britain, whose Blairite avatar started resembling the Tories. In democratic politics, sending confused and confusing messages to one's core electoral base is simply not a smart thing to do.

An undercurrent of Hindu anxiety was developing on account of well-publicized mass conversions to Islam like the ones in Meenakshipuram in 1981, that seemed to be funded by money from the Gulf. Around this time, the BJP was also helped by the clumsy mistakes of the Congress party. The oft-repeated formula that in politics it is always safe to wait for the opponents' mistakes came to the BJP's rescue. After the disastrous Shah Bano episode, when the Congress passed a law depriving a poor Muslim divorcee of the compensation that the Supreme Court had granted her, the Congress had painted itself as the party that appeased Muslims, and that too Muslims of the most loud, traditionalist and obscurantist variety. The Congress went one step further and handed something to the BJP on a platter. The Congress reopened a hundred-year-old Ayodhya dispute that had been buried in the courts. And what an issue that was! It concerned the purported birthplace of Lord Rama, who is so central to the entire country's consciousness. Such opportunities come infrequently in the political life of democracies. They resemble a tide in the affairs of men, and the BJP certainly took the tide at its flood.

Free India had moved quickly to settle scores with the erstwhile British rulers. It was easy to at least make sure that the humiliations of a couple of hundred years were no longer constantly assaulting our senses. Statues of British emperors were removed and sent to the junkyard. Prominent thoroughfares which had previously been named for British viceroys were now named for local heroes. The names of the three great presidency towns of the Raj – Madras, Calcutta and Bombay – were summarily changed.

But that did not deal with the questions arising from earlier conquests, dominations and humiliations. What were we to do with sacred sites where possibly triumphalist monuments had been set up, where earlier structures had been erased or set aside? In Banaras, the Maratha queen Ahilyabai Holkar had built a temple right next to Aurangzeb's mosque, which had been constructed on the site of a holy temple, using in part the stonework from that temple. In Mathura, during the Raj, Hindus had set up a temple right next to the idgah that Aurangzeb had built on the site of an earlier magnificent temple established during Akbar's reign by the Raja of Orchha.

But Ayodhya, the traditional birthplace of Rama, was different. No Maratha queen had ventured there. No side-by-side compromises had been made during the many decades of the Raj. In the town of Ayodhya, the Nawab of Oudh had faced frequent troubles and riots. But he was a Muslim ruler, even if he was relatively tolerant and even if he was of the heterodox Shia persuasion. Within a short while after Dalhousie's annexation of Oudh, the Hindus of Ayodhya were back with both public demonstrations and legal actions. They felt, in Bankim's mode, that British rule represented an opportunity for them to revive their earlier lost cause. But there was no resolution in favour of the Hindus.

In the period immediately following Independence, the Hindu politicians of Awadh seem to have concluded that a fait accompli could help them get back the sacred site that they hankered for so much. They made some progress as they were able to set up a small shrine adjacent to the Mughal mosque. Once this had been accomplished, the matter disappeared into the labyrinthine maze of the Indian court system.

In the 1980s, the Congress government persuaded the judiciary to make relaxations in favour of Hindus by opening up a small shrine in one section of the Mughal mosque. The question immediately arose: why should there be only cosmetic relaxations? Why could there not be a magnificent temple dedicated to Rama at his purported birthplace, a site which had been snatched away by invaders who preceded the British? This became the slogan and the platform that the BJP brilliantly capitalized on. The BJP was helped by the fact that our dreary state-run monopoly TV network all of a sudden decided to serialize a Bollywood version of Rama's tale seen through the eyes of Ramanand Sagar, who will probably go down in Indian cultural history as a figure as important as Valmiki or Kamban, Tulsidas or Tyagaraja.

The BJP put together a well-crafted national programme in support of the proposed Rama temple. The party organized a motorcade, referred to as a rath yatra, from different parts of the country to Ayodhya, leveraging the Mahatma's political technique which had demonstrated that a slow pilgrim's march is a winner in Indian politics. The BJP also used the Rama temple movement very intelligently on the caste front. The volunteers in the marches and motorcades came from all castes. Dalit volunteers were specially honoured as layers of foundation stones. The BJP had successfully broken away from the accusations of its critics that it was an upper-caste

Brahmin–Bania party. The late Kanshi Ram had always lampooned the communists in India as having upper-caste leaders and lower-caste foot soldiers. The BJP, consciously or otherwise, avoided this pattern. Lower-caste and Dalit leaders, like Ram Nath Kovind, who was later to become the president of India under the BJP government of Narendra Modi, emerged, and the century-old Lajpat Rai dream of Hindu consolidation was pursued with a sure touch.

The denouement of the temple movement came on account of mob violence, which the Uttar Pradesh state government had solemnly assured the Supreme Court would not happen. The inability of the Hindu nationalist forces to control extreme elements remains problematic for conservatives. The criticism that this was not so much a result of inability but of conscious unwillingness makes it more ominous. Some societies recover from events like the anti-Catholic Gordon riots in England in 1780. Others are met with a whiff of grapeshot that then degenerates into tyranny, which is what happened in France when the glorious French Republic was replaced by an empire which turned out to be a Bonaparte family enterprise. The tendency of extremists, with or without leadership support, indulging in violent and destructive action remains an Achilles heel and has the potential to convert a regular political movement into a mob-driven affair, the consequences of which could be extremely bad indeed.

~

Almost imperceptibly, the face of Hindu nationalism changed. Gone was the opposition to English and the attempts to force Hindi on reluctant states. Traces of obscurantism associated with the revivalist ideology were quietly jettisoned. The Ram Rajya Parishad's opposition to changes to the Hindu Marriage and Divorce code would appear quaint today. Hindu nationalism has acquired a chic, contemporary edge. Technology was leveraged and the electronic media was embraced. Hindu nationalism found new intellectual and financial support from the Indian diaspora who became champions of Indic pride and self-assertiveness. The BJP continued to capitalize on the Congress's mistakes. Narasimha Rao's economic liberalization had unleashed fresh energy in the economic sphere. An aspirational, or at least wannabe, upwardly mobile population was emerging, which soon numbered in the millions.

Given that Rao was the architect of liberalization, the Congress should have claimed these voters as their constituency. But the Congress pointedly failed to do so. In fact, Rao is today seen as more of a quasi-BJP hero than the lifelong Congressman he was. Sidelining Rao and his achievements is one more costly mistake of the BJP's political opponents, which suited the BJP's political strategy.

Finally, the BJP managed to come to power in the 1990s. But it was caught in a trap very similar to what it faced in the 1970s, when the Jana Sangh was part of the Janata experiment, and in the 1980s, when the BJP was flirting with Gandhian socialism. The compromises required by coalition governments resulted almost always in the loss of a sharp-edged identity. It became fashionable to state that there was no difference between the Congress and the BJP. This allowed the Congress a ten-year comeback, often in coalition with the same smaller parties that had worked with the BJP.

~

And then came Modi. It is always difficult to be objective about contemporary issues or personalities. But let us make an attempt at analysis. Modi is not from Uttar Pradesh, Maharashtra, Vidarbha, the Punjab or Bengal – the traditional homes of Hindu nationalist leaders. Modi is most definitely not from the upper castes – Brahmin, Rajput or Bania. The BJP publicity machine has made sure that his backward caste origin is well known. The

Bhandarkar–Lajpat Rai dream of an overarching Hindu identity that effectively leaves caste behind can only have credibility if genuine, not symbolic, leadership finally passes to someone who is lower caste by birth and who makes it on merit. Modi symbolizes precisely this. He comes with a track record in state administration, and in that he resembles Morarji Desai, V.P. Singh, Narasimha Rao and Deve Gowda. His Hindu nationalist credentials are in no doubt whatsoever. But that is not his core political message. Modi is arguing, both subtly and not so subtly, for an aspirational and achievement-oriented Indian society with a strong Hindu flavour. The repeat motif is that India's time has come. Providence has given India the opportunity to make itself prosperous, strong and great, and here is a monastic, dedicated hard-working leader who represents this opportunity. And in the pursuit of national goals, Modi demands of his followers important sacrifices. The path is not an easy one, but a tough one. Bankim could not have said it better. A content analysis of Modi's speeches reveals the virtually unbroken connection with *Anandamath*, where Bankim highlights the importance of sacrifice and effort in order to re-energize Mother India.

The question is whether this new version of Hindu nationalism passes the conservative test. It is definitely market friendly but, arguably, not sufficiently market friendly. A move away from an intrusive state that has disdain for voluntary contracts would have been more palpable if the previous dispensation's retrospective taxation law had been abandoned and if there had been greater genuine, instead of cosmetic, privatization. But on the other hand, if we favour gradualism, this step-by-step embrace of the markets may not be such a bad thing.

On cultural matters, there is a refreshing approach, grounded in empiricism. Despite continued activity by the anti-Macaulay elements in the social media, the BJP government has had no hesitation and has felt no embarrassment in openly embracing many aspects of our Raj legacy. We have connected with Belgium, France, Israel, Britain and the US in honouring Indian veterans of the First World War and Second World War. The earlier canard that these Indian soldiers, sailors and airmen were mere mercenaries or wicked collaborators has been openly dropped. Pandit Nehru had argued that persons of Indian origin in East Africa should think of themselves as Africans and not Indians. Today, there is no hesitation in welcoming and embracing the diaspora. The introduction of the Pravasi Divas and the Pravasi awards are unique BJP contributions.

~

The gradual replacement of Marxists and their fellow travellers from our academia is a particularly optimistic outcome. They are being boxed in. They squeal a great deal. One hopes that steadily, methodically and inexorably they are marginalized. A friend has made an argument that the replacements for these appointments are both unqualified and obscurantist. I am tempted to take the position that anyone, even the most unqualified and obscurantist person, is better than Marxists, or for that matter Freudians, postmodernists and their other charlatan friends.

But on second thoughts, one has to concede that this would be a self-goal. Burke, Hume and indeed large chunks of Anglo-Saxon thought have been conspicuously excluded from academic curriculums. Mention of the Tirukkural or the Shanti Parva, of the purusharthas, charitra or Yuga Dharma results in the professor being dismissed derisively as a reactionary.

Removing names and ideas from texts and curriculums is an idea first pioneered in Berlin and Moscow. The fact that Indira Gandhi's and Nurul Hasan's followers have done it subtly and slowly does not make the outcome less lethal. PhD students have been encouraged to practise idolatrous worship at the altars of the most recent icons of Western intellectual fashions like Foucault and Derrida. Indian history is taught as nothing more than a sinister upper-caste hegemonic conspiracy. And all this has been going on for decades with the full support, blessings and patronage of American and European academia. The net result is that, except possibly in economics, there are virtually no people who can be appointed to replace the usual sample of dim-witted leftists.

What does one do? I feel a considerable amount of sympathy for our university appointments committees. Their task is difficult. But appointing obscurantists who shoot off silly comments about non-existent ancient Indian greatness is not the answer. A diligent, methodical and comprehensive faculty search process is the only possible plan of action. Difficult tasks require effort, focus and energy. We must proceed with the full conviction that these changes are required for fulfilling the promise of our Yuga Dharma.

The focus on connectivity, transport and tourism is an interesting attempt to recreate the magic of India's pilgrimage circuit in modern terms. Emphasis on tying up traditions with commerce and tourism by focusing on textiles, handicrafts and local festivals are quite heartening. Cultural and literary festivals organized by voluntary efforts in several towns, not just in metropolitan centres, are an emerging phenomenon, which must warm the hearts of conservatives.

~

On social matters, the BJP's record appears more mixed. Continued attempts at Hindu consolidation across castes has meant that there is some softening in the caste system. The religious angle has been more problematic. Emphasis on the ban on cow slaughter and cattle transportation has resulted in extreme elements indulging in mob violence. The argument that there have been no major riots or state-sponsored violence is a strong one, but it is not a sufficient one. Conservatives can never go along with tolerance for mob violence. This remains a question mark and a source of anxiety.

The reaching out to Sufi Muslims and smaller groups like Bohras represents an interesting contrast. It is as though Hindu nationalists are now taking an interest in looking at Indian Muslims not as a monolithic entity, but as a part of Indian diversity. The outreach to Muslim women who are seeking to free themselves from discrimination and persecution is also an interesting one. But the jury is out as of now. How the BJP manages these tensions, which can be both creative and destructive, will be interesting to watch.

Within the Hindu nationalist movement itself there remains an ongoing tension between those who push for economic growth and technological progress, both of which demand a certain amount of accommodation with Western and global influences, and those who are more concerned with temple building, temple rituals, cow protection and opposition to genetic technologies. This might become the real problem for Hindu nationalism in general and for the BJP in particular in the days to come.

An aspirational class that likes modernity but is also comfortable with diverse traditions is the key growing political constituency. Catering to this constituency, which views politics instrumentally, may require the toning down of Hindutva and embracing modern technology and growth-oriented economics. This is precisely where the creative tension arises. Discarding sharp identity positions like Hindutva can result in the core electoral base losing interest. In the 1980s, the BJP opted to tone down Hindutva and adopt a woolly-headed doctrine called Gandhian socialism. Going into the 2004 election, it appeared that the BJP was not that different from the Congress. This may have led the hard-core Hindutva-oriented electoral base to be less enthusiastic than they would otherwise have been. Another source of ongoing tension is the fact that despite recent successes in the north-east and in the east and inroads in Karnataka, large parts of peninsular India still present challenges for Hindu nationalism. The challenge of dealing with multiple tensions and trade-offs leads to the possibility that Bankim's vision of a regeneration of the Hindu collective gets attention only sporadically and episodically and not in a sustained manner.

Modi's second victory is in some ways too recent for us to fully understand or evaluate. The step-by-step extension of Hindu nationalism across all regions is noteworthy. The continued partial success in creating a pan-Hindu identity that seems to finally be overcoming horizontal and vertical caste barriers is also a measure of the distance Hindu nationalism has come from Bankim's days. Modi's victory acceptance speech rather unexpectedly introduced the 1857 motif. In 1857, Hindu and Muslim sepoys had emerged as a 'band of brothers' against a common adversary. It's almost as if Modi had read the historian Rudrangshu Mukherjee's account of this event. But Modi did not have to go there at all. He could have stuck to Savarkar. The early Savarkar had written about the common national nature of the 1857 rising. It was Savarkar who had first referred to the events as the first war of independence. Modi seemed to be going back to the intellectual traditions begun by Savarkar, albeit the early Savarkar, not the later one.

It is one thing to create a 'band of brothers' feeling across complex identity groups like Hindus and Muslims in a warlike situation. Will Modi try to do it in peacetime conditions? If he does, will he succeed? Will Muslims in large numbers react positively, especially in the context of the events of the last thirty years? In the process, could Modi end up alienating his core supporters? All of these are imponderable and fascinating questions. The answers will finally come to historians of the future. We will be witnesses or sakshis to events and the trends as they unfold.

~

From the point of view of the Burke–Rammohun Roy school of conservatives, the best approach might be to opt for the Rajni Kothari strategy of trying to influence caucuses within other parties. A revival of the Swatantra Party does not appear to be a practical proposition. This is why Swatantra stalwarts like S. V. Raju adopted a pro-BJP stance. The best bet for Burkeans might be to influence the caucuses, elements and groups within the BJP that see India as a natural member of what the Anglo-American writer the late Christopher Hitchens and the Canadian critic Mark Steyn refer to as the emerging Anglosphere. The key to doing this is to make the case that the English language, English common law, and institutions of the Raj which still have constructive characteristics associated with them need to be preserved, protected and enhanced, while in no way succumbing to orientalist contempt for the rich tapestry of our culture – what the great Kannada writer Maasti referred to as 'bahuratna vasundhara' or the earth studded with many gems.

To sustain this argument, we need to repeatedly make the case that given the commonalities inherent in the human spirit, there is a rare confluence between Tiruvalluvar and the Shanti Parva on the one hand, and Burke and Adam Smith on the other. Tiruvalluvar and the Shanti Parva are focused on the good life of the individual in the social context requiring categorical imperatives on the part of both the individual and her larger community to participate in the harmonious pursuit of all the three goals of such a life – economic and political activity, activity associated with beauty and the passions, activity informed by virtue and ethical conduct. And all of these were to be tested in the world of empirical reality and distilled in the minds of the ploughman, the merchant, not just the king. Burke and Adam Smith were concerned with both the individual and society attempting to satisfy the moral requirements of a conscience represented by an impartial spectator, while seeking material welfare through voluntary organic systems and processes, and avoiding royal or aristocratic tyranny, all these efforts informed by the wisdom of common people. Both these sets of thinkers from different parts of the world emphasized the obligations of the people of every period to their ancestors and to their descendants.

Conservatives have to try and influence the elements within the BJP who subscribe to Burke's call for changing in order to conserve. We need to stress that rejecting the historical legacy of the Raj is not only not smart, but it goes against the views of Bankim and Vivekananda that there was something providential about that association. Conservatives are likely to meet with resistance from the anti Macaulay-putra lobby within the BJP and its affiliates. Nevertheless, this effort must not be dropped. Sometimes I tell people that the bachelor Macaulay was a reborn Rishyashringa, who propitiated the gods in order to ensure that King Dasharatha was blessed with a son. Just as that young bachelor Rishyashringa blessed us all by ensuring the birth of Prince Rama, so too has Macaulay blessed this land.

Conservatives must also diligently, persistently and emphatically keep warning the nationalist leadership that militancy, violence and mob actions have devoured political movements in the past. One can even leverage the legend of Bhasmasura, who while successfully burning his enemies ended up burning himself. This, in all likelihood, will strike a chord.

The same Rajni Kothari strategy of influencing parties from the outside can and perhaps should be followed in the approach that conservatives take with regional parties. One can argue that precisely because of their linguistic and caste identity markers, the Trinamool, the DMK, the ADMK, the JDU, the JDS, the SP, the BSP, the BJD, the NCP, the Shiv Sena, the SAD and the AGP can be influenced from within and without to be more market friendly in economic matters, more anti-Marxist in cultural matters, more in favour of gradual sustainable reform in social matters and supporters of the Magna Carta ideas of liberty and the rule of law in political matters.

Given the very limited intellectual articulations within these parties, this seems an uphill task. But it is interesting to note that at least on economic matters these parties are not opposed to markets. They would prefer that markets are rigged in favour of their financiers. But at least they do not support mindless statism, if only for practical considerations. Their regional, linguistic, ethnic and caste foundations ensure they will not adopt sterile Marxist materialism. On social matters, even as they fiercely defend the interests of their identity groups, they have demonstrated maturity in their approaches. The BSP is particularly intelligent in not attacking Hinduism, but only its Manuvadi component. This automatically implies a commitment to preserving the good things of the past, presumably in their mind, the non-Manuvadi components of our traditions. The Trinamool has as its slogan 'Ma, Mati, Manush'. How can any conservative argue against this? Attempts to gently persuade the Trinamool to take their own slogan seriously and to move in a conservative direction are not looking as though they will succeed, given the increasing volatility in the party's tactics. But the attempt must be made.

~

The recent electoral setbacks of the communists should not result in conservatives becoming complacent about them. Marxists continue to have a disproportionate influence in Indian academia, especially in the departments of the humanities and the social sciences. By many accounts, they routinely gang up to deny appointments, tenure and promotions to conservatives. They are at the forefront in the efforts to brainwash students into believing the Indian state is an oppressive one. Their narratives regarding Kashmir, the north-east, the tribals of central India, Dalits and Muslims are full of cockamamie exaggerations.

The Indian state is routinely portrayed by Marxists as a fascist and totalitarian entity. Modern Hinduism is depicted as nothing but an ongoing upper-caste, patriarchal conspiracy. They never seem to give up on their Leninist aspirations of wrecking bourgeois democracy from within. They routinely support vicious subnationalist movements, which are prone to ethnic cleansing, oppression of minorities and mindless violence. They do not want to admit that if the so-called Kashmiri liberation struggle were to succeed, the fate of Buddhists, the remnant minuscule Hindus, Ahmadiyyas, Shias and for that matter Kashmiri Sunni women, who would face Islamic state restrictions, would end up being horrifying. Their narrative completely ignores the fact that the 'brave' Naga and Mizo national liberation struggles are brutally cruel towards Meiteis or Bors.

Above all, they refuse to understand the imperial nature of the modern Indian state, which like the empire of the Hapsburgs preserves a unity with a light and deft touch among numerous ethnic groups. There is not a single state in India, including the ones in the north-east and for that matter Kashmir, which does not have multiple minorities that would be at risk if India breaks up like Yugoslavia. Sarajevo and Srebrenica will end up looking like tea parties. We have the experience of the horrors of the 1947 Partition and the 1971 civil war in the erstwhile East Pakistan. While they may pretend otherwise, it is crucial that we remind their gullible students in taxpayer-funded universities that under the instruction of Comrade Stalin, the communists of India supported Partition and that their great Chairman Mao supported Yahya Khan's genocide in Bangladesh.

Using their fifth-column implants in the Planning Commission, they ensured that India was programmed for poverty, even as East Asia went ahead. Their numerous agents who continue to oppose markets, which are the best hope for India's prosperity, need to be countered. After 1989, they have focused a great deal on cultural matters, and their favourite words are hegemony and deconstructionism. They do not subscribe to the idea of India and would be happy with the dissolution of the Indian state and the complete fragmentation of Indian culture.

It is the bounden duty of conservatives to raise the needed warning signals. For every Krishna Menon they try to plant in our midst, we must ensure that we have at least a Rajagopalachari and a Masani. For every Nurul Hasan, the Marxist fellow traveller whose awful legacy has been the semi-permanent conversion of the humanities and social science departments of our universities, we must have a B.R. Shenoy, the intrepid free market economist who lost the battle in his times only to emerge a hero later, and a Nissim Ezekiel, who never compromised in his defence of liberties even in the darkest permit licence raj days.

~

What about the Congress party of today?

Many are arguing that the grand old party is no longer grand. It has lost ground by staying focused on outdated statist and socialist policies, not paying heed to aspirational India. This I would argue is not a good reason to ignore the Congress. Politics can take many unexpected courses. The Congress should not be written off, if for no other reason than that it has considerable salience and contributes disproportionately to the intellectual dialogue in Indian politics. Can conservatives try and influence the grand old party from the inside and the outside? On economic matters, certainly the Manmohan Singh camp within the Congress is open to being market friendly. Even if this caucus appears to be somewhat weakened right now, there is every reason to believe that it can and will make a comeback. Conservatives need to maintain the pressure on this group.

On cultural matters, the Congress seems to have veered away not only from Nehru and his love for the Ashoka Chakra, an enduring symbol of our culture and not susceptible to fashionable deconstructionism, as well as the Maheshamurti at Elephanta, one of Pandit Nehru's favourite sculptures where Shiva is not treated as a Hindu embarrassment, but also from Indira Gandhi and her passionate attachment to the *Atharva Veda*, which she frequently quoted in order to make the point that the spirit of environmental conservation is deeply embedded in our country right from Vedic times.

It is almost as if the Congress is in love with academics in Indian, American and European universities who have converted rootlessness into a legitimate state of affairs, and who are interested in pursuing the Churchillian argument that India is merely a geographic expression like the equator. Oddly enough, the scion of the Patiala dynasty, Amarinder Singh might emerge as one of the better hopes within the Congress of reigniting a sense of pride in Indian culture and traditions. M.A. Sreenivasan and Mirza Ismail, those gifted servants of princely India, may have been prophetic: Amarinder Singh's intrepid presence makes the case that perhaps there is indeed great value to monarchical memories and traditions.

On social matters, the Congress party has tied itself up in some difficult knots. The idea that a minority group can have a first claim on national resources is startling, and opposed to respect for the majority and to a shared mutuality of national interests, both of which Scruton emphasizes. The Congress ideologues seem to want to move to the position that we are nothing but a country of minorities. This might work in the US, which was built on ideas. But in India, where shared sacred geography and centuries of shared traditions (I have written on these themes in Chapter 3) are so central, this simply will not fly. Such an approach to our society might, in the opinion of some, result in short-term electoral gains. It could also backfire. The baneful influence of left-wing academics over the Congress party seems to preclude at this time the creation of any caucus inside, which might be of use to conservatives, at least on this dimension. Nevertheless, the attempt should not be given up.

Our best allies may be the marketing and media managers within the party. We need to keep reminding them of Scruton's seminal insight that the majority needs not only not to be ignored, but it also needs to be respected. As persons at the end of the day in contact with voters who are the ultimate customers and consumers of politics, I believe that they will understand. On no account should conservatives ignore the Congress party. It may not be the dominant party of old. But it still represents a very important and vital vertex of political articulation. We must influence from without and encourage the conservative caucuses within.

~

Before I end this section on politics, it is appropriate that I touch on the issue of corruption in India. Corruption itself is a universal phenomenon that does not respect borders. As the economics Nobel laureate Gary Becker says, 'Crime always pays.' The corrupt are excellent bookmakers. They estimate the probabilities carefully. If the expected value of the gains from crime and corruption exceeds by orders of magnitude the expected value of losses, fines or punishments, then corruption becomes a logical act, at least from a utilitarian and not a conservative perspective.

The government of free India has made it worse. It has systematically introduced laws and regulations that require citizens and businesses to get approvals, permits, licences, quotas, subsidies, drawbacks and no-objection certificates from dozens of departments and agencies. India is the only country I know of where the expression NOC or no-objection certificate exists. The result is that the Indian state acts as a gatekeeper, a toll collector and a tax gatherer, not only for the benefit of the state itself, but also for the benefit of its functionaries. The Indian official and the Indian politician have boarded a gravy train that sucks the blood of its people in general, and its most entrepreneurial people in particular. This has resulted in great economic costs. We would be a more prosperous country and our people would be less impoverished by orders of magnitude if only corruption were less. We don't even have to eliminate it or reduce it greatly. Even a modest reduction would suffice. While the Raj certainly tolerated some corruption, free India has made an industry out of it. Rajagopalachari repeatedly pointed out the fact that the so-called planned economy was corroding us morally and debilitating us economically. That has surely come to pass.

The recent public perception that there has been a significant decline in corruption in high places has not addressed the structural issues associated with pervasive bureaucratic and political corruption at all levels in our country. Using technology in order to provide benefits to the poor directly bypassing the state's venal functionaries is a good move. But it does not deal sufficiently with the fact that the administrative apparatus of the state on the ground is intrusive, oppressive and corrupt. In other words, in more places than we care to concede, the residues of the inimical permit licence raj are still around. This is the source of phenomena like 'tax terrorism' and 'inspector raj' that we frequently hear of. We need comprehensive administrative reform including police reform and judicial reform, adhering to the conservative requirement that these are in fact the primary functions of the state and that these need to be both efficient and honest. In the absence of such reform, Indian citizens will continue to be victims of a capricious state where corruption remains an old and familiar friend.

~

Let me also talk about a worrisome socio-cultural issue affecting politics. One of my friends calls it the Dhritarashtra complex. This is the ability of otherwise intelligent persons of high integrity to have a blind spot when it comes to their children and families. There seems to be no end to the wealth people accumulate for their families, no end to the nepotism and favouritism involved, even if this goes against the public weal. Here is an area where we might wish to study the ancient Romans, who put the commonwealth first. This might be an important attribute we need to cultivate and acquire, gradually, but with a certain determination if we wish to remain a successful and civilized republic.

On balance, political conservatism in contemporary India needs to accept that an outright revival of the Burke–Rammohun Roy–Swatantra tradition is unlikely to succeed. However, the battle to try and plant conservative ideas in existing political formations and to steer them in that direction is one that has sanguine prospects. The continued evolution of the Hindu nationalist conservative position on pragmatic, empirical lines, an acknowledgement of the diaspora and a possible position for us in the Anglosphere is certainly a source of optimism. A century ago, the Kerala conservative Sankaran Nair warned the Mahatma that civil disobedience and hartals could lead to anarchy. The dangers of mob action remain a definite risk. Regional parties, despite their rather quaint utterances, should not be written off. They can be sources of unusual, if limited, optimism. And it is a mistake to write off the Congress as a leftist den. In the past, conservative caucuses within the Congress have worked in fits and starts. That tradition needs to be strengthened. India's grand old party remains a challenge and an opportunity.

3

The Cultural Sphere

Now to step away from the heat and controversies of politics, to consider the equally complex subject of culture. Indian conservatives have had to deal with a foundational question: is there such a thing as Indian culture? If it exists, is it recently imagined in the manner described by the American scholar Benedict Anderson, for whom the advent of modern technologies like print and mass media are critical for the emergence of ideas like nationalism? Or is 'Indian culture' something which has been around for centuries, having a respectable tradition going back in time? This is particularly important because of India's size, geographical diversity and historical discontinuities. It is easy to forget that sixteen medium-sized European countries can be squeezed into a scale map of India. It is also a fact that no Indian monarchical institution shows a firmly and coherently recorded unbroken continuous chronology. England can claim to have a continuous monarchy from the year 1066 CE. France can claim to be a continuing nation from 508 CE. India has had many kingdoms, empires and dynasties with several breaks along the way. Continuity is one thing that has been conspicuously absent. Does this absence of political continuity mean that there is no enduring ancient Indian culture also?

Both foreign and Indian scholars frequently tell us that it is outsiders who refer to us as Indians. This would imply that there is no indigenous imagined idea of India with any degree of antiquity. Marxist and post-colonialist scholars have come up with a new kind of orientalism. They pretty much agree with nineteenth-century British administrators and missionaries that not only was the political unification of India entirely a British affair, but the emergence of a so-called Indian national culture was simply the result of British rule and had no earlier roots whatsoever.

The high Sanskritic version of Bharatavarsha – extending from the Bridge on the Ocean to the Abode of Snow – as a definite geographic idea going back in time was dismissed then by British members of the Viceroy's Council and is now dismissed by academics. This Sanskritic imaginary is seen as a defensive upper-caste Hindu elite response to the contemptuous dismissal of their claim by Western Enlightenment votaries and Christian missionaries. Even the Ramayana and the Mahabharata are rejected as pan-Indian projects. And the Bhagavad Gita is positioned simply as something that desperately diffident upper-caste Hindus needed to exaggerate and deify to show that they too had the equivalent of a Bible, which the new conquerors possessed. Wendy Doniger, who is enormously influential in both American and Indian academic circles, peddles this view. That the Bhagavad Gita was considered a part of the prasthana-traya or three authoritative texts of Vedanta some thirteen centuries ago is glossed over, because anything to do with Shankara, the founder of the school of Advaita Vedanta, is doubtless characteristic of Brahminical hegemony. We should simply ignore such commentators, whose objective is to caricature rather than to describe. They are not endowed with earnestness and sincerity, which Krishna suggests in the Gita is a requirement for a good student.

~

The nineteenth-century European views of India were also deeply coloured by a theory that upper-caste Indians were the descendants of Indo-European Aryans who had gone native in India by intermingling with Dravidian, Mongolian and Austric races. Such intermingling and the enervating climatic conditions of the Indian peninsula had presumably turned the Aryans into a bunch of weak, effeminate losers. On this theory was overlaid one more, of Aryan race oppression being at the root of India's caste system, justifying an aggressive counter-response from those who were quite arbitrarily classified as descendants of a Dravidian race. As it turns out, the Dravidian race theory seems to have been almost single-handedly invented by the activist Protestant missionary Reverend Caldwell in the nineteenth century.

The subaltern school of Indian historians may not have intended it, but their studies that emphasized diversities and the need to go beyond dynastic and elite narratives have come in useful for a wide variety of Marxists and crypto-Marxists to dismiss the idea of an overarching Indian culture, not necessarily by any factual analysis, but by indulging in value-laden criticism, referring to all attempts at defending an indigenously imagined and ancient Indian culture as simply an exercise in trying to reassert upper-caste, Brahmin–Rajput–Bania, Hindu, patriarchal, exploitative, quasi-racist, wannabe Aryan hegemony. They miss the point that the discussion is about culture and not about religion. Not just the Ramayana and the Mahabharata, but the Jataka tales too need to be viewed as part of the ancient palimpsest of Indian culture.

The anti-Hindu bias comes in handy for those who wish to demolish the idea of an ancient Indian culture with a semblance of unity. The political case for this is simple: if an ancient Indian cultural unity is denied, then we are left with a territorial state following frontiers defined by the British. This mere geographic entity need have no integrated cultural persona, a position that suited orientalists then and suits postmodernists now.

Colonial semantics defined Hindus as a religious group. Would it have worked differently if Hindus had been defined as a cultural group? We should not fall into this trap. We are talking about an enduring Indian or Indic culture that is not to be left to the mercy of the vocabulary of arbitrary classifications that our critics have control over. We must pay attention to the fact that Indonesia and Thailand are able to view the Ramayana as part of their cultural heritage. One is a largely Muslim country and one is a largely Buddhist one. But when it comes to India, we get shy and embarrassed to acknowledge any affection for the Ramayana, because our texts get classified as religious. Gurcharan Das was actually confronted in Delhi salons when he talked about his interest in the Mahabharata. The chatterati of our capital city asked him contemptuously if he had become a Hindu fundamentalist. Note the derision for the Mahabharata and the embarrassment involved in even calling someone a Hindu. I would argue that the best response is to ignore such foolish questions. Let us remember the British conservative philosopher Roger Scruton's position that respect for the traditional culture of the majority, however we choose to define the majority, is not something to be ashamed of. It is something to be cherished.

The Indian conservative response to the colonial stereotypes and the more recent Marxist and post-modern orientalism has been sensitive, sensible, intrepid and firm. Even Pandit Nehru, who can hardly be called a person of the conservative persuasion, had his moments of conservative epiphany. His conversations with the French intellectual and public figure Andre Malraux, his introspections while sitting on the steps of the Borobudur temple in Java, his luminous last will and testament, and quite simply so much of his writing, show him up to be one who would have argued vociferously that the idea of an Indian culture is solid and is ancient.

Being sentimentally attached to the Vale of Kashmir and to Allahabad, Pandit Nehru could not escape a north Indian geographic bias. Tagore, who hailed from the eastern frontiers of the peninsula, had a more interesting approach to dealing with the challenge of diversities. He simply acknowledged them, even celebrated them.

Bauls, Vidyapati, Vaishnava lyrics were all important for the Bengali bhadralok poet. At the risk of making a personal intrusion, I would like to narrate a story. When my grandparents visited Tagore, the poet spent the major part of an evening discussing Mysore and Tanjore veenas and the importance of making sure that both rosewood and jackfruit-wood veenas were produced. Tagore celebrated India's diversities. He wrote his short story 'Hungry Stones' when he was visiting Ahmedabad in Gujarat, and he set 'Jana Gana Mana' to music when he was visiting Madanapalle in Andhra Pradesh, and in so doing affirmed India's unity. Mind you, he did this not in a chauvinist way, but with the solid conviction that India had something peaceful, creative and constructive to offer to world civilization.

The European argument that cultures were coterminous with nation states with hard frontiers, single languages, homogeneous inhabitants and preferably one religious confession was a political one. And that is the argument used by British administrators against a political formation known as India. Very well. We simply agree. We invoke Tagore's spirit. We then go on to make the case that the Indian cultural rubric we speak of exists despite no political unity, despite no hard frontiers, despite no homogeneity in the population, despite no linguistic uniformity or even religious denominational closeness. That is the aha moment for those of us who imagine an indigenous foundational Indian culture of considerable antiquity. We do have an Indian culture and we describe it and celebrate it in our vocabulary and if we are not able to convince Indian Civil Service officers, Anglican missionaries or tenured professors at American universities, then quite frankly, that is their problem, not ours.

~

The classical Sanskritic ideas of a culture that permeates the geography of the peninsula will not disappear because Western scholars and their Indian acolytes do not like them. Consider our myths – or to use Pandit Nehru's melodious expression: 'legend, myth, story and song'. Rama, Sita and Lakshmana stay on the banks of the Godavari at a place called Panchavati, which we now call Nashik. Rama enters into a dialogue with the King of the Oceans, at Darbha-shayana and at a spot a few miles away called Rameswaram, he worships Shiva. He is the same prince who has come all the way from Saketa on the banks of the Sarayu. Bhima and Arjuna wander all over the land that we call Bharatavarsha, marrying different damsels and promoting a raunchy national integration that of course will be condemned by our critics as badly patriarchal – but never mind. And even the name Bharatavarsha – does it come from the Bharata tribe or from the son of the beauteous Shakuntala and the not so likeable Dushyanta? It is the land where blackbucks roam, tigers rule, peacocks strut, lotuses bloom, mangoes blossom, jasmines suffuse our olfactory nerves, koels call and where the krauncha bird inspires Valmiki, our adi-kavi or primal poet.

And it is not only in the realm of myth that we make claims to antiquity. Let us consider history. Why would a Rashtrakuta king in modern Maharashtra and a Pallava king in modern Tamil Nadu build a temple for Shiva who is worshipped all over our land, and refer to Shiva as Kailashanatha, the Lord of Kailasha, which is in the distant northern Himalayas? And these temples were not built as a response to British rule or on account of Western inspiration. They were built some fifteen hundred years ago. Why would Tamil poets refer to Krishna's abode as vada-Madurai, the northern Madurai, and not just as Mathura? Why would Andal, the great Tamil poetess and quasi-divine figure, recreate some fifteen centuries ago a Gokul in Srivilliputtur in the distant south? And of course, whether Marxists agree with us or not, we hold that some thirteen centuries ago Adi Shankara established religious institutions in the extremities of Bharatavarsha – Joshimath in the north, Sringeri in the south, Dwarka in the west and Puri in the east. In recent times, the brilliant writer and political commentator Pavan Varma has written a book where he has captured the romance and the febrile energy of Adi Shankara with great aplomb. We hold that some ten centuries ago Ramanuja went all the way from Kanchipuram in Tamil Nadu to Sharada in Kashmir, which is now a ruined village on the other side of the Line of Control, to obtain a well-preserved manuscript of the Brahma Sutras, and some eight centuries ago the great Vedantic Acharya Madhva went from Udupi in coastal Karnataka to Badrinath in Uttarakhand.

Does all this sound too Sanskritic, too Brahminical and too hegemonic? Then just consider the fact of the pervasive diversities embedded in our traditions, which effortlessly encompass tribal groups who British census commissioners and phrenologists casually categorized as belonging to a different race. The art historian Pupul Jayakar points out that whether it is Savara attendants at the Jagannath Puri temple or the Ayyappa temple at Sabarimala in Kerala, the name of the mythical tribal woman Sabari from the Ramayana rings down all the way from legend to our lived experiences today. Instead of accusing upper-caste Sanskritized Hindus as conspiratorial creators of an imagined Indian culture in order to get over their inferiority complex vis-à-vis their British rulers, and as hegemons attempting to marginalize tribal people, perhaps we should consider the alternative theory that tribal populations were and are central to Indian culture, and that marginalization, if any, happened at the hands of British administrators, and the myth of marginalization suited the ideologies of evangelizing missionaries.

~

Orientalists and their contemporary intellectual descendants argue that the idea of Indian culture is articulated only in Sanskrit, which of course is a dead language. The argument goes forward to suggest that today Sanskrit is just a medium for upper-caste Hindu indulgence in sinister nostalgia. We need to reject this completely. This imagined idea of India as a cultural unity is widespread in virtually all Indian languages. In the early twentieth century, the Tamil poet Subramania Bharati talked about an Indian commonwealth when he referred to 'Bharata samudayam'. In the mid-twentieth century, Kuvempu's *Ramayana Darshana* in Kannada reminds us that every age, every place has a rendering, a vision and a view of India's unforgettable prince. Maithili Sharan Gupt proved that point again when he rewrote the Ramayana in Hindi through the eyes of the prince's younger brother and his wife.

My favourite example of the overarching interconnectedness of Indian culture across centuries and across languages is the story of the Great Flood and the first humans. The Great Flood or pralaya has resulted in waters covering the whole earth. The fragile remnants of humanity float on a leaf that enables them to avoid drowning. As the waters recede, they have to start the human journey once again. This haunting theme is captured in Sanskrit in the *Markandeya Purana* more than a thousand years ago; it was resurrected and reimagined by Allasami Peddanna in Telugu some five hundred years ago and reborn in a different way in the Hindi verse of Jaishankar Prasad in the twentieth century.

~

The next argument that we need to deal with is the religious one. Is all of this talk of the sacral contours of Bharatavarsha too Hindu and exclusive? Does it not demote to a secondary status Indians who do not subscribe to Hindu beliefs and who cannot be Hindu pilgrims? This is one of those trick questions where our intellectual adversaries hope that we will get defensive at first and then go on to a shrill, aggressive posture. My view is that we can soberly, calmly and quite easily refute this argument.

It is not just Hindus who visit holy places across the

land and who are obsessed with seven holy towns and seven sacred rivers. Holy hills, holy spots, holy waterbodies seem to be obsessions with all varieties of Indians. We are aware of a Jain pilgrimage circuit that exists today, which covers Jharkhand, Bihar, Rajasthan, Gujarat, the west coast and southern Karnataka. The Sikh circuit goes from Amritsar, or perhaps more correctly from Nankana, across our current western border, through Anandpur and Delhi and Hemkund all the way to Patna in the east and then south to Nanded in west-central India. The Buddhist circuit, which had gone dormant for centuries, now covers Sarnath, Gaya, Amaravati, Nagarjunasagar and, for several contemporary Indian Buddhists, a sacred site in the centre of the country in Nagpur, along with one in the western city of Mumbai. Given its long history in India, Islam has evolved its own sacred geography within the frontiers of Hind. I have a Muslim friend in Delhi who is of the Sufi persuasion. Every few years he completes a pilgrimage circuit within India – starting in Delhi, going west to Ajmer, then south through Ahmedabad, Mumbai, Gulbarga all the way to Nagore in the deep south and then back north through Cuddappah, east to Patna and then back through Fatehpur Sikri to Delhi. This is the sacred Sufi circuit, all within current territorial India. Merely by calling it Hind and not Bharatavarsha, clearly the land seems to become no less holy. Incidentally, it appears that India is the only country where there is such a sacred Sufi Muslim geographic pilgrimage circuit.

The imagined idea of a holy parikrama or perimeter can transcend religious hurdles. It constitutes evidence of the existence of an overarching Indian culture so strongly denied by seemingly omniscient Marxist and postmodern academics. When I see Catholics rushing off to Vailankanni and Sardhana, not to forget Goa and Bandra, and Parsis making a trek to Udwada and Sanjan as part of a renewal of their earliest Indian memories, I for one am persuaded of the fact that our imagined Indian culture firmly embraces the idea of pilgrimages within our own territorial geography.

The idea of Mother India, we are told, started a hundred-odd years ago with Bankim and Abanindranath Tagore in Bengal. And then, we are assured by the new orientalists that there follows the familiar story of upper-caste Hindus with an inferiority complex having the need to salvage their self-respect playing their usual games and embracing this newly invented, rather than ancient, idea of Mother India. It is one more of those assertions that begin to acquire an aura of truth through sheer propagandist repetition.

Uncannily, the art historian Richard Blurton in an entirely different context makes the case that even in ancient and medieval art the land of India itself was seen as the body of the mother goddess. Even the mountains and rivers of the land are features of her holy body. Perhaps this was the source of inspiration for Bankim's resonant lines in his 'Vande Mataram'. Legend has it that when the body of the great goddess was cut into pieces, it fell in places as far off as Kamakhya in the north-east in Guwahati, Hinglaj in the distant west in Baluchistan in territory beyond our current frontiers, Kanyakumari in the south and Vaishno Devi in the north and in numerous spots all across the length and breadth of the country as we know it.

Diana Eck is a pleasant rarity among American academics; she seems to have a rare sensibility that enables her to feel a mystic connect with India. She presents a brilliant insight when she talks of the goddess at the southern tip where three oceans wash the feet of the land itself, standing as an auspicious guardian.

Mother India as defining the sense of our cultural collective unconscious ends up having interesting ramifications. The psychologist and writer Sudhir Kakar, who has delved deep into psychological issues associated with Indian culture, sees the mother figure as more central for us than for many other cultures. How this phenomenon, including veneration of the female figure, can persist along with extremely anti-feminine social practices is something that remains puzzling and which needs examining when we discuss social issues. Salman Rushdie, in his brilliant novel *The Moor's Last Sigh* makes the point in his inimitable way: 'India is a major mother country'.

But the most fascinating insight in this area in recent times has come from the maverick polymath scholar Ashis Nandy. Nandy notes that in our imperial encounter with Western Enlightenment, our British rulers characterized Indians in general, and Hindus in particular, as cowardly, weak and effeminate. Western scholars and their Indian students have assumed that such a psychological attack by our conquerors constituted a thesis, which must have resulted in an antithesis on our part, in accordance with the theories of the German philosopher Hegel. Hence everywhere Western observers look for responses by diffident, shamefaced Indians trying to make themselves copies of their rulers, mostly with dismal or comic consequences. Kipling's Bengali Babu, for example, with his Oxford degree, tries to give a riposte to the British. But his inherent unmanly cowardice makes him a caricature of an Englishman. Nandy rejects this view of the world. In the personality of Mahatma Gandhi, Nandy sees the calm acceptance of the feminine in himself and by extension of the feminine in all his countrymen and countrywomen. There is no Hegelian antithesis here. There is instead a welcome mat laid out to the hyper-masculine rulers and hyper-analytical scholars of the West to engage with the feminine in us and in themselves and head towards an androgynous denouement.

It can be argued that the pursuit of the androgyne within each of us at the individual level and by Indians as a collective might end up being one of the most creative of responses to the challenges posed by the human predicament. In accepting, embracing and celebrating and definitely not feeling ashamed of the ardhanarishwara, or the androgynous god within himself, within all of us, the Father of Our Nation quite consciously reaffirms one of the most ancient and enduring symbols of our civilization.

The Indian challenge to British rulers is of considerable philosophical interest in a wide variety of contexts. The Mahatma challenged the British that they were not being faithful to the best in their own traditions as represented in the Gospels of St Mark and St Matthew. He went further when he casually and disdainfully rejected the association of cowardliness with the feminine self.

Indeed, the conquered land and people of India showed their rulers an interesting mirror: they could look to their own bard, Shakespeare, who captured androgyny beautifully in the characters of Rosalind, Portia, Imogen and Viola. Setting portraits of these Shakespearean characters side by side with gorgeous images and icons of Lord Shiva, who combines the masculine and the feminine within each one of us, might constitute something infinitely better than a trite Hegelian response – it might be the ultimate challenge to the prejudices and stereotypes propagated by our British rulers to recognize the common humanity that the rulers and the ruled share. Nandy makes the point that despite being the weaker conquered lot, the Indian response, perhaps because it is touched by the sacred, has heroic, constructive and creative dimensions.

It is important that in making a sober and enduring argument about the legitimacy of Indian culture we not fall into traps. Examples of these traps are: when were the Vedas written? Were Aryans originally from India or from elsewhere? Were the Vedas composed by the same people who built cities on the banks of the now vanished river Saraswati? Were there fights between Buddhism and Hinduism? Which came first: this or that? And many other such debilitating exercises in wading through quicksand. My simple point is that these are red herrings. None of these issues are relevant for rejecting the argument that some people keep making, that the idea of India is unreal, at best recent, and almost always reactive and reactionary. That position is plain wrong.

~

So what does this so-called Indian culture, whose idea I have been defending, consist of?

First, it is concerned with the sacred. Indian culture can never be based on a purely materialistic construct. Neither can it revolve around a purely human idealism. It asserts, many times effortlessly and unselfconsciously, that humans have a connection with something beyond themselves. The currently ignored A.L. Basham, author of *The Wonder That Was India*, an outsider, has understood it and puts it simply: we Indians believe in a transcendental reality beyond the mundane that we deal with every day. And we have no problems dealing with the paradox that this so-called transcendental reality is in fact a creation and a creature of our own minds.

Because the attachment to the 'sacred' is so central to Indian culture, it is worth drawing attention to the fact that it is genuinely pan-Indian across geographies, languages, religions and ideologies. What always fascinates me is the frequent assertion by pilgrims that Vishnu pervades the universe. But he is particularly fond of Tirupati, Puri, Dakor and Guruvayur, among thousands of other special sacred spots. The goddess commands the universe. But guess what, she likes Vindhyachal, Danteshwari, Jwalamukhi, Ambaji and Madurai with a special love. And that is not to forget the very special love for Gamdevi or Mahalakshmi, which are spots close to where I live. Shiva of course is simultaneously a cosmic person and a resident of Banaras, Rameswaram, Triyambakeshwar and so on.

One simply cannot run away from the sacred in India whatever one's ideas or ideologies. The engagement with the sacred exists even amid unlikely ideologies, like Indian materialism, though one would expect that materialists have no need for the transcendent or the sacred. The Charvaka school of Indian materialism too rejects simple-minded hedonism and opts for a sensitive concern with the sacred.

Even with the influx of so-called modernity, India and Indian culture continue to stay suffused with the sacred. Every year, in Puri in Odisha, hundreds of thousands of pilgrims come to witness a sacred procession, when the images of Jagannath and his siblings are taken out. I am not suggesting that there are no religious processions in other parts of the world. But virtually all observers are agreed that the collective epiphany experienced by the huge crowds in Puri during the rath yatra is quite unique. The writer William Dalrymple makes out a similar case about the annual 'wedding' of the goddess Meenakshi and Shiva in Madurai, which he says is a profoundly moving recurring ritual that goes back thousands of years. Madurai is not a city with a temple – Madurai is and will remain the sacred playground of the goddess Meenakshi, and this sacred association is once again accepted and embraced effortlessly. For yet another example, I suggest a visit on a Thursday evening to the Nizamuddin dargah in Delhi. The qawwali, which incidentally is unique to our subcontinent, is performed and all the visitors to the dargah, of different faiths, experience a communal tryst with the sacred. Only in India!

~

The arguments put forward by followers of Freud, that India's obsessive interest in the sacred is simply a result of sexual repressions or indulgences, should not receive much credence. However, the unfortunate fact is that universities in the West and even in our country routinely teach along these lines. Let me narrate an anecdote to you. In an exchange of correspondence with my friend the celebrated neuroscientist V.S. Ramachandran, he had this to say: 'Freud's views are considered poppycock in mainstream neuroscience.' We went on to discuss the Parvati–Ganesha legend as well as the hundred-year-old Tamil kriti 'Enna Tavam Seydanai Yashoda' composed by Papanasam Sivan and set to the raga Kapi. Sivan asks a vital question, at least one that is vital for us: 'What penance did you do, Yashoda, that the Lord of the Universe was willing to appear as your child and call you Amma and willingly let himself be tied up?' To argue that Yashoda and Krishna were in a suppressed incestuous relationship, or that the guru–shishya relationship between Yama and Nachiketa in the *Katha Upanishad* was about repressed homo-eroticism and not about seeking wisdom, merely because a Freudian researcher says so, would in Ramachandran's words 'be equivalent to arguing that Macbeth is not a magnificent commentary on the human condition, but a superstitious story on witchcraft and ghosts'.

My assertion of our age-old and, in our vocabulary, karmic connection with the sacred needs no defence. But it certainly could do with a rejection of ridiculous intrusions based on discredited oracles. The pseudo-savants Marx and Freud may have hurt their own cultures by their disdain for the sacred. Thank you very much, but we are not willing to let them hurt ours.

Second, Indian culture genuinely believes in diversity of the spirit. Even the most tyrannical patriarchal Indian husband will not stand in the way of his otherwise servile wife having an ishta devata, or preferred manifestation of the divine, different from his. Her soul is her own. And again, this transcends religious boundaries. Only in India can a Sunni Muslim husband live with an Ahmadiyya wife. Only in India can a Parsi be a devout follower of Shirdi Sai Baba, or a Hindu try to seek wish fulfilment at the Nizamuddin dargah or at the Vailankanni basilica. And when Sheik Chinna Moulana played the Karaharapriya raga classic 'Chakkani Rajamargamu' on the nadaswaram, when Ustad Abdul Karim Khan sang 'Rama Nee Samaanam Evaru', when Mohammed Rafi sang 'Madhuban Mein Radhika' set to Naushad's music, and when today Yesudas sings 'Venkatachala Nilayam', you understand the real meaning of the expression 'diversity of spirit'. Observe that quite recently India submitted the film *Lagaan* for the Oscars as representative of our country. That film's soundtrack includes a composition 'Radha Kaise Na Jale', which was composed by A.R. Rahman, with lyrics written by Javed Akhtar, in which the fickle Krishna is portrayed by Aamir Khan in a dance choreographed by Saroj Khan. Many may have heard the classic T.M. Soundararajan song 'Paattum Naaney' in the movie *Tiruvilayadal*. Lord Shiva, who is the patron of Madurai city, supposedly sings it. The lyricist Ka Mu Sharif wrote the song. He certainly qualifies to be a Shiva devotee. These examples, at a minimum, completely demolish the myth that religion is a barrier to common expressions of Indian culture.

The art historian Partha Mitter has noted that nineteenth-century Europeans found it difficult to appreciate the extraordinary fecundity and the baroque excesses that characterized the walls and towers of Indian temples. The idea of sculpting or painting divine figures with sixteen pairs of arms was even seen by some of our conquerors as grotesque and as going against Western classical norms of simplicity.

The problem, I would submit, is not with our sculptures, but in the eyes of the beholders. Because they were accustomed to the Venus de Milo or the musculature of Michelangelo's David, they found the four-armed Chola Nataraja or the three-headed Kalachuri Mahesha or the Mamallapuram Pallava Durga excessive. They just could not see that excess, difference and variety was the counterpoint to the unity that our philosophers sought and apparently sometimes found. The art critic Coomaraswamy makes the case that the aesthetic encounter with an Indian painting or sculpture is nothing if it is not simultaneously a spiritual encounter also.

Even a casual visitor to India invariably remarks on the diversity of colours, sounds and smells, on the entire range of senses being attacked and sometimes overwhelmed. It is our destiny to live with, among and around this diversity. This is perhaps what one of India's greatest twentieth-century writers, Maasti, meant when he extolled our land as 'bahuratna vasundhara'– the earth studded with many gems. And I submit to you that it is something worth cherishing.

Third, Indian culture is comfortable with paradoxes. In

fact, we positively enjoy paradoxes. Not for us the logical proposition that two mutually exclusive possibilities cannot exist simultaneously. In fact, the Jain idea of syaadvaada specifically asserts the possibility of multiple, mutually contradictory positions all being simultaneously valid and true.

An argument can be made that this attachment to paradoxes results in a lack of a scientific temperament given to experimental verification and replication. It also permits a set of spurious, pompous obiter dicta that can pass off as wisdom. These criticisms have an element of validity. But it must be pointed out that even as Indians have loved playing games with paradoxes, we have allowed practitioners like Susruta to perform intricate surgeries and empiricists like Aryabhatta to calculate eclipse occurrences with astonishing accuracy. Even practitioners of astrology who believe in shadowy planets and frozen horizons will fall back on Aryabhatta's accurate astronomy to fix the timings of eclipses.

It is worth thinking about whether the embrace of paradoxes does or does not contribute to greater psychological health.

Binary and exclusionary approaches can lead to conflicts that end up never getting resolved. Engaging with paradoxes helps inculcate tolerance and acceptance of differences and dissent, and thus makes it easier to be comfortable living with conflicts without letting the conflicts overwhelm us.

Fourth, Indian culture can combine personal austerity with collective indulgence in joyful pursuits. Many of our heroes and role models are persons who have become sanyasis, fakirs or ascetics. Possibly the greatest child of our land, the Buddha, chose to abandon his palace, his wife and his child and went to the forest after shedding his hair in search of enlightenment, which we are told he obtained. According to tradition, another great philosopher and mystic, Shankaracharya donned the ochre robes of an ascetic despite his mother's anxieties with his decision. The abiding indwelling passion to abandon the world and to seek its meaning in ascetic isolation remains a recurring and haunting theme in our culture. While we do have traditions of organized monasteries, the tradition of the lonely anchorite is the one that keeps popping up. This seems to stem from a concern with dealing with the primal and fundamental conundrum of consciousness. This permeates a wide variety of oral and textual traditions ranging from the *Mandukya Upanishad*, the Fire Sermon, Jnaneshwari, Tiruvachagam, all the way to the writings of Ramalinga Vallalar. To this day, it remains fashionable both in popular schools like Vipassana and in the unsurpassed insights of Ramana, considered by many to be the ultimate consciousness guru of the twentieth century. Why austerity needs to be a prerequisite for pursuing enquiries into the realm of human consciousness is a question that I personally have not been able to answer. This is not the proper place to deal with this recurring theme.

What we can and should consider is that the emphasis on ascetic isolationism has led to the unfortunate conclusion that joyful and meaningful this-worldly pursuits are not important for us. This as it turns out is far from being true. India is the land of festivals and festivities. Every season, every month, every day in the lunar cycle can portend a festival that involves colour, music, dance, frivolity, feasting and sheer joie de vivre. One needs to only look at the sculptures of festive processions etched in stone in Bharhut, Khajuraho or Hampi to realize that this attachment to collective enjoyment has been with us for ages. The Ganapati and Durga festivals, which in their current form are fairly recent, derive their inspiration from ancient practices. The brilliant painter Sooriyamurthy captured in the twentieth century on a long canvas a set of singers, drummers, flautists and dancers in a procession of wild abandon. While his faces have a cubist tinge, the legacy of our ancient bas-reliefs and temple walls cannot be missed.

The best explanation for the balance between austere asceticism and joyful playfulness has been made in recent times by the philosopher Anthony Parel and the writer Gurcharan Das, who go back all the way to the doctrine of purusharthas or the objectives of humans in this life, not in the next world. Ancient texts like the Shanti Parva of the Mahabharata and the Tirukkural devote extensive and intensive attention to artha, or the pursuit of economic and political well-being; kama, or the pursuit of passion and the pleasure principle; and dharma, or the pursuit of virtue and ethical thoughts, words and deeds. Curiously enough, the fourth purushartha of moksha, or the pursuit of salvation, is ignored both by the Mahabharata and the Tirukkural. In these texts, we are confidently and a tad mischievously informed that pursuing the three worldly goals well would automatically take care of salvation. So much for Indian other-worldliness!

The Apastamba Sutra of the *Yajur Veda*, which the historian P.V. Kane dates to the fourth century BCE, talks of Yuga Dharma – the virtue or the ethic that is appropriate to the age. It is Parel's case that Mahatma Gandhi in his own inimitable way figured out that in the present yuga, it makes sense to walk away from the excessive emphasis on moksha that prevailed in earlier times, and to substitute it with emphasis on the other three purusharthas and to consider service to fellow humans as a dharmic necessity. It is not accidental that although he referred to his establishments as ashrams, he did not set them up in distant forests or mountains. He set one up on the then outskirts of a city and another bang in the middle of the country. The dharma of Gandhi's times demanded an active involvement with this world, with his country, with his city.

~

To describe Indian culture in a few paragraphs, making a limited number of arguments, is of course a travesty of sorts. Suffice it to say that the very argument of the diversity of our spirit makes this a non-starter. The idea of embedded diversity within an overarching persona needs to be emphasized to demolish the arguments of postmodernists who would like to simply propose an anarchic landscape of many cultures. The twentieth-century polymath Shivarama Karanth did make the case for recognizing differences and pluralities in order not to fall into the trap of chauvinism. But in all humility I would assert that this reinforces rather than rejects Maasti's argument: the existence of 'bahuratna', or many gems, in no way suggests that vasundhara, or the earth, is split likewise. The principal points that need to be made are that there is a thing known as Indian culture; it has been imagined not in recent times, but over millennia; it has distinct characteristics and it can survive and transcend arguments, however valid, of its having a casteist or patriarchal bias. Above all, Indian culture is wrapped up with the sacred and diverse geography of India.

Jews have an attachment to the Promised Land, stretching from Dan in the north to Beersheba in the south, and they have a culture whose legitimacy no one questions. Every Englishman knows or should know that their first major literary work engages with the geography of England, and that too a sacred one. Geoffrey Chaucer's *The Canterbury Tales* is all about a pilgrimage within England. And of course, as the great English poet William Blake attests, the saviour Jesus Christ himself walked in England's 'green and pleasant land'. The legitimacy of Englishness, a distinct English culture, all the way down to the Beatles and Harry Potter, remains unquestioned.

Merely because we in India have a history of being conquered, and in recent times one set of self-appointed arbiters see us as Marxist or Freudian objects with no original thoughts of our own, does not mean that we will give up on our 'tryst with destiny'. The Indian conservative stand is that in spite of the lack of a tradition of hard political unity, despite our diversities, and precisely because we are exuberantly immersed in our diversities, we are possessed of an overarching interconnected cultural persona. While definitely heavily Hindu, this cultural persona goes beyond the merely Hindu in religious terms; which while beholden to Sanskrit, embraces all our languages; and which is possibly upper caste insofar as the culture of any country or people tends to have a class bias.

Rajagopalachari, who remains a versatile giant in the Indian conservative pantheon, wrote a prose version of the Ramayana in Tamil and called it 'Chakravarti Tirumagan'– the Holy Son of an Emperor. He then wrote a prose version of the Mahabharata and called it 'Vyasar Virundu', the Feast of Vyasa. Both are considered classics of Tamil prose and reflect a chaste and limpid style. He then collaborated with a friend to translate both these works into English. And in the language of our erstwhile rulers, both of them have become enduring classics. There can never be an end in our land to the telling and retelling of the story of Rama and of the fratricidal war of the Mahabharata.

The contemporary English philosopher Roger Scruton is immersed in history, religion and aesthetics. Scruton has chosen to engage with the Christian religion and related aesthetics like church music and church architecture, even if such pursuits are currently unfashionable. He has put up a convincing defence of English culture. In India, we need a Scruton lookalike. Given India's unending engagement with the sacred, Scruton as a source of inspiration would be appropriate. One can only hope that there is a budding Scruton among the young people in this country. This conservative thinker needs to be one who rejects the jejune superficial analytical methodology of shallow materialists and superficial psychobabblers in their Marxist, postmodern or Freudian forms. They should instead derive their inspiration from the anirvachaniya or inexplicable Parabrahman or Supreme Being whose energy pervades the universe, but who specially blesses India!

4

The Social Sphere

Conservatism in social matters is a sort of Achilles heel. Caste oppression, untouchability, oppression of women and marginalization of tribals are seen as central and inescapable when it comes to our social traditions. Defending tradition, which is an inherent conservative impulse, becomes difficult and allows our opponents to demonize us. We need to fall back on the thoughts and words of a great hero of modern conservatism, who is sometimes forgotten. The archetypal English conservative statesman Benjamin Disraeli argued convincingly that it is not the case that conservatives want to preserve everything of the past. What conservatives seek to do is preserve the 'best of our past', not its worst aspects. On this score alone, Indian conservatives in the past two centuries have had no problems with the position that Indian society has been in need of substantial, even foundational, reform. It is interesting to see how many of our genuine reformers have actually been in the conservative mould. Rammohun Roy, who was by no means a radical revolutionary, set the stage. Roy was a political conservative who supported British rule. At the same time, he campaigned against sati. And his campaign had a Machiavellian cleverness about it. He took recourse to the argument that sati, in fact, had no scriptural sanction among the Hindus. This is not the place to deal with the arcane arguments made by him and his adversary Radhakanta Deb. It is the place, however, to note that appealing to earlier traditions, casting them with a pristinely ancient halo and leveraging the situation to jettison so-called more recent accretions to tradition is an argument that many conservatives have made.

Gandhi did something similar. While paying lip service to the so-called varnashrama doctrine, which presumably sanctioned rigid heritable caste differences, he did everything possible to sabotage caste and debilitate fatally its most extreme feature: untouchability. Some would argue that Gandhi's patronizing approach to Dalits, whom he referred to as Harijans, smacks of the hypocrisy that invariably accompanies the honeyed words of representatives of the ruling class. Cynics would argue that his attack on untouchability was a mere tactic of convenience designed to protect his vote bank. Conservatives know better. Frontal attacks on existing traditions run the risk of encouraging destructive Jacobins who, in this case, along with abolition of sati may resort to pulling down all Devi temples and abolishing the Bhagavad Gita.

Disraeli knew a thing or two. We need to make sure that even as we jettison the worst aspects of our past, we do it with care.

In *A Tale of Two Cities*, Charles Dickens has created a fascinating character called Dr Alexander Manette. Manette denounces the brutal aristocrat Marquis de St Evermonde. At the same time, Manette saves the life of the Marquis's son, who has changed his name to Charles Darnay. Dickens was making the case for attacking the bad features of the French aristocracy, not for wholesale killings. As a matter of fact, the French revolutionaries did not follow Manette's example. They discarded and destroyed without restraint. This resulted in all the baneful consequences of the French Revolution, which Edmund Burke so brilliantly exposed in his *Reflections on the Revolution in France*.

The social reformers Mahadev Govind Ranade and Maharshi Karve were political moderates. And yet in their opposition to social practices like child marriage and discrimination against widows, they achieved much. One could even argue that they achieved much more in constructive terms than rabid rabble-rousers who criticized without offering practical solutions.

The most interesting attempts at social reform have come from some groups of so-called Hindu nationalists who are usually not given enough credit for this. The Arya Samaj not only allows but also encourages and enjoins its women adherents to participate in Vedic rituals, something that was taboo for traditionalists. The Arya Samaj also rejects caste. The same Samaj through its DAV schools encouraged English education as a liberating force. It is significant that the middle word in DAV, Dayanand Anglo-Vedic, is 'Anglo'. Instead of being praised for these positions, virtually all the academic literature on the Arya Samaj produced by our university intellectuals remains focused on the so-called dark nature of the Samaj's Hindu nationalism.

In recent times, the Vishwa Hindu Parishad (VHP) has recruited Dalits as volunteers to lay the foundation stones of Hindu temples. Again, it is easy to dismiss this as some kind of malevolent symbolism. Why not take the high road and actually appreciate it? Or is it simply the case that good reformist ideas are only palatable if they come from those who look down on anyone who calls herself a Hindu?

On the thorny issue of caste itself, two very interesting intellectual developments need attention. The first is a view that economists like R. Vaidyanathan and historians like Chhaya Goswami have drawn our attention to. While it is true that the caste system is not what Disraeli would refer to as one of the better features of our social traditions, it is also the case that caste may be playing a valuable role as a lubricant of economically efficient networks and hence enhancing social human capital. The astonishing successes of the Nadars of Sivakasi, the Gounders of Tiruppur, the Jains of Palanpur, the Marwari Banias of Rajasthan, the Bunts of Dakshina Kannada, the Dawoodi Bohras and the Patels of Gujarat and so many other caste groups in mobilizing themselves for business development and growth would suggest that not all the effects of the caste system are necessarily undesirable. I for one am watching with great interest the recently formed Dalit Chamber of Commerce and rooting for its success in creating a strong network enabling this group of entrepreneurs to make their mark.

The second development is something that can only be called the reimagining of caste history. When a caste association consciously posits the existence of a glorious past, focuses on its great leaders and creates an aura of pride around the caste identity, this serves not only a political purpose, but it also moves society towards a greater acceptance of the equality of castes rather than the traditional assertion of hierarchies. It is in this light that we must see the efforts of someone like Mayawati to create monuments and parks celebrating Dalit leaders. In a curious way, this helps create a level playing field.

My friend the learned historian Father John Alphonse Correia used to say that Indians drink in caste with their mother's milk. This ancient malady, if that is what it is, seems to stay with us forever, even as it alters itself considerably. During the days of the Raj, the decennial censuses gave it a new contour. Castes tried to position themselves as higher in the gradation every ten years. Today, castes are running helter-skelter to position themselves as more backward than each other, to avail of quotas for dwindling government jobs. In either case, the phenomenon of caste itself seems to refuse to disappear.

Ambedkar and Rajagopalachari had it right about caste, just as the English historian Toynbee had it right about race. The former two argued that in the long run it is intermarriage alone that can lead to the disappearance of the strange social stratification of caste. Toynbee argued that American racial differences and hierarchies would only finally disappear with intermarriage among the races. Intercaste marriages are certainly increasing in India. But I would hesitate to predict the death of an institution as enduring as caste.

The fundamental problem that a full-blooded individual-loving conservative has with caste is the phenomenon of prescribing an identity to the individual on account of her birth, with insufficient concession to the inherent rights and responsibilities of the individual. The consequences are baneful. Imagine a glove-maker's son in Stratford being told that he could never write plays; he had to content himself all his life with making gloves. Nearer home, imagine where our republic would be if a Mahar had been denied an education simply because he was a Mahar. We would be the losers with a less classy Constitution. My favourite writer from our distant past, Tiruvalluvar, we are told, did not hail from the Brahmin caste, which by no means then or now had or has a monopoly on intellect. Incidentally, in Tiruvalluvar's weltanschauung, or world view, it is the ploughman who is central to society. Let me give you a rough and inadequate translation from Tiruvalluvar: 'He who tills the land and eats the fruits thereof, he alone lives. The rest of us are mere free-loading camp-followers.' The English poet Langland has given us a brilliant poem: 'Piers Plowman'. Perhaps Tiruvalluvar had reached Langland through some long-forgotten translation. Or perhaps, as is more likely in human affairs, geniuses separated by time and space have amazing experiences of serendipity and synchronicity.

The irony is that the Ramayana and the Mahabharata repeatedly make the point that inherited caste is not a good marker for talent, ability or even moral uprightness. And yet, these tales are overlooked, and caste survives and prospers in India, even as it mutates into different forms.

The consequential damages from the suppression of free human capital development are a huge social cost and might be among one of several reasons why our society has not achieved the economic breakthroughs that should have happened.

The second problem with caste is that it creates needless hierarchies in occupations and among social groups. This leads to the loss of territorial solidarity among people inhabiting the same village, the same district, the same country. This is ironic, because territorial solidarity across Bharatavarsha, as I mentioned earlier, is so central to our national consciousness.

The conservative belief that gradual social change, which came to us perhaps through the proverbial providential agency of the Raj and which has continued in free India, is something that happens below the radar screen, but that it has emphatic consequences struck me the other day when I visited the registrar's office in Mumbai. As you are all doubtless aware, we in India are privileged to have many registrars and sub-registrars who are presumably busy registering and sub-registering something or the other. On one wall of this august office were five photographs. They were of Shivaji Maharaj, Ambedkar, Jyotiba Phule, Savitribai Phule and Shahu Maharaj. These presumably are the current heroes and role models of Maharashtra. Interestingly, none of them are Brahmins. And at least a couple of them espoused anti-Brahmin positions. Gokhale and Tilak are absent, not because they were not eminent, but because they were Brahmins. This happens in a state where a mere two hundred years ago, under the Peshwa-shahi, Chitpavan Brahmins were the dominant ruling class. Change happens. Change has happened. A systematic, slow, osmotic de-Brahminization of our polity, or at least of our registrars' offices, has occurred and continues to trundle along. Western anthropologists like Louis Dumont, who wrote elegantly about the frozen nature of India's caste system, have been proved wrong.

The caste system evolves and continues to evolve. Having said that, one must acknowledge that as someone involved in the game of prediction, it is perhaps unwise to forecast the complete demise of caste. We can and we should wish for continued change. As persons committed to the gradual improvement of Indian society, we must hope for this change to be in a positive direction. As conservatives, we have to live with the hope that the excessively dysfunctional features of the caste system will get moderated, that Indian human capital will benefit from the emergence of talented individuals from different backgrounds and that a modicum of solidarity will emerge among individuals, for individuals are the central subjects we are concerned with.

~

The so-called mistreatment of tribals by Indian society is a bit of a calumny that has now acquired the character of an established truth. It is important for us to assert that unlike the white settler societies of North America and Australia, Indian society has not attempted to destroy hunter-gatherer groups and then lock them up in museum-like reservations. Settled agricultural Indians have lived side by side with hunter-gatherers and swidden cultivators for millennia, and there have been astonishing levels of commerce between these societies. The exchanges have been both economic and cultural. I do not want to belabour this point. I will ask you to just consider two examples. The tribals of India have given us some of our most beloved gods – Jagannath in Odisha, Vitthala and Khandoba in Maharashtra and Ayyappa in Kerala. In Srisailam in Andhra Pradesh, to this day, the temple of the goddess Bhramaramba is given over to the Chenchu tribals one day in a year, for she is their special kinswoman.

And not just in traditional religious matters does this phenomenon exist. Consider twentieth-century Indian painting. What would Jamini Roy have done if he had not converted himself into a tribal?

In contrast to these creative engagements, we have seen considerable tribal alienation in independent India. I would argue that this is because we have failed to leverage conservative leaders like the Munda tribal politician Jaipal Singh and Pravir Chandra Bhanj Deo, the erstwhile ruler of Bastar who fought for the rights of tribal people in his state. We have instead preferred to focus on top-down state-driven, bureaucracy-led patronage, which almost invariably gets transformed into corruption and oppression.

But this too shall pass. Tribal alienation is fanned by some Marxist ideologues. Encouraging tribals to combat the Indian state is a truly suicidal prescription. The approaches of cultural activists like Kamala Devi Chattopadhyaya and Pupul Jayakar were any day more constructive. You get a feel of this constructive approach when you visit the Museum for Tribal Arts in Bhopal. I am optimistic that our ability to engage with diversity will eventually prevail, and superficial imported ideologies like Marxism will meet the death that they deserve.

～

On matters of gender, the situation in our country where female feticide is rampant, where neglect of the female child is the rule and female participation in the labour force is low, we are confronted with yet another feature of our traditions which conservatives cannot and do not defend. I wonder how many know that one of the early supporters of female education and increased female entry into the workforce was the great engineer-statesman Sir M. Visweswarayya. Other conservatives who devoted much of their lives to these matters include Cornelia Sorabji and Sivaswamy Aiyar. Again, by not focusing on constructive engagement, but by indulging in shrill sloganeering, defenders of feminism might actually be diverting attention away from practical reform. It is a much more difficult task to provide training, employment and dignity to women than to sit in coffee houses and write tracts on patriarchy which are read by a small coterie of admirers.

There is a managerial view based on the principles of central planning that technology is morally positive. Conservatives have always been wary of these quasi-utopian fantasies. It is three decades since amniocentesis and ultrasound were introduced into healthcare facilities. And in these decades, our female to male ratio has dropped precipitously. Systematic killing of female fetuses along with systematic neglect of the girl child has resulted in this awful consequence.

The low female ratio in our population is one of the consequences of easy abortions, an idea that was forced upon us by the central planners of the UN who told us for years that we needed to have a national state-sponsored population control programme. Our approach to abortion was not based on feminist arguments or on the fact that illegal abortions would happen anyway and would create more tragedies. Our approach was based on insidious state intervention. This debate has been settled by our usual method of passing an ineffectual law that using ultrasound for sex determination is illegal. It might be worth checking how many convictions have resulted from this worthy law.

The demographic consequences of the state aggressively pursuing birth control, at the behest of the central planners of the World Bank and the Ford Foundation, are the creation of other time bombs for our country. Some states are more vigorous in implementing this rather dubious programme. The relative populations of states are changing and we have to resort to playing tricks with adult franchise as we freeze parliament seats on the basis of an outdated census.

The frequent public arguments about the differential rates of birth control adopted by different caste and religious groups is another mischievous and dangerous time bomb which is the direct result of the state trying to get involved with this most intimate and private of human decisions. All of this is rooted in the central planner's strong belief that left to themselves the poor will breed mindlessly and that the state has to intervene. A more gratuitous insult to poor human beings, merely because they are poor, is difficult to imagine. Recent state intervention supporting the girl child by way of a public campaign is at least sensitive and sensible. It is a source of minimalist optimism.

Too often, we try to cover up our social weaknesses and failures in the realm of gender relations by pointing out that we have many successful women, or that our laws are pro-women, and that we are much better than Pakistan. These are self-evidently weak arguments. The British philosopher Roger Scruton repeatedly makes the point that institutions, allegiances and traditions need to adapt. Please note that changing laws are a necessary but not a sufficient condition. In this, Scruton echoes Burke, who said: 'we must reform in order to conserve'. In our case, we could even think of revival in order to go back to the best in our earlier traditions, rather than the worst in our recent ones.

The best results seem to come from voluntary efforts by people. Muslim women are spearheading the movement for female entry into the Haji Ali dargah. Parsi women are fighting for the right to perform the navjote for children born to non-Parsi fathers. Dalit women are leading literary movements, pointing out that Dalit men who seek betterment can frequently be miserly in granting similar consideration to Dalit women. I am impressed that in the heart of traditional Pune we have a bunch of women Hindu priests. My daughter Sanjeevani took the position that ancient Hindu texts allowed for the sacred thread to be very much a woman's right. The Rammohun Roy trick of appealing to earlier scriptures in order to jettison more recent discriminatory social practices continues to be relevant and effective.

All these movements and changes, however small in scale and however episodic, do contain the germs of reforms that Burke and Tiruvalluvar would have independently favoured.

On the other hand, state intervention through the judiciary and the executive is backfiring, apropos the Sabarimala controversy. The injection of political heat has not been helpful. One must hope that recently invented anti-women traditions, which are suddenly being given an antique glow, are countered effectively and that social reform does not get stymied. Let us not forget that societies that do not harness their full human capital potential end up as losers. At a moral level, the continued oppression and stigmatization of women stinks in our nostrils.

~

Current concerns with human sexuality turn out – at least in India's case – not to be that current after all. One of the finest arguments in support of transgenders is by my friend the sculptor Dilip George Kuruvilla. Every year, he visits the Aravaan temple near Villupuram in Tamil Nadu to attend a festival where transgenders get together to get married to their god Aravaan, who according to them is none other than the divine son of the divine Arjuna. Kuruvilla's hyper-realist fibreglass sculptures of these marvellous devotees of a cult that goes back hundreds of years represent androgynous elements within each one of us, in the most authentically Indic and universal idioms. The point I am trying to make, if not already clear, is that we do not need to engage with LGBTQ issues only in the language of the Upper East Side or the Rive Gauche. As Indian conservatives, we have the good fortune and privilege to dive into our own cultural wellsprings to find inspiration, comfort and calls to action. And as we have already discussed, if it is Indic, then the touch of the sacral and the sacred is inevitable. It is interesting that in the public discussion in recent times on LGBTQ rights, columnist after columnist, even those not of the conservative persuasion, found it useful to play the Rammohun Roy trick: deride recent accretions in tradition and argue about going back to earlier ones.

~

The social attitude of India's rich and powerful, irrespective of their castes, regions or faiths, is something that we cannot dismiss. It is central to our behaviour as a people. Foreign observers as far apart as Aldous Huxley and Alexander McCall Smith have noted it. An insider–outsider like Naipaul has referred to the 'layer on layer' of cruelty that characterizes Indian society. It took a Naipaul to notice something that you and I have become blind to. The poor in India, those who wait on us, those who carry our bags, those who look on us with a mixture of fear and resignation, they almost invariably have thin legs. The maverick Pakistan-born Canadian politician Tarek Fatah has said somewhere that every time he has visited India he has witnessed the rich and the powerful shout at the poor.

Conservatives need to worry about this both for practical and for moral reasons. Going back to Charles Dickens's *Tale of Two Cities*, one remembers an incident where a poor child is killed in the Paris neighbourhood Quartier St Antoine. The child is crushed by the carriage of a callous aristocrat. When the revolution comes, the residents of that neighbourhood take their revenge on the aristocrat's family. There is a lesson there for India's rich.

Till now, India's rich have possibly benefited from the karmic fatalism and the inherent peaceable traits of our poor. This did not last forever for French aristocrats, who were guillotined during the French Revolution. The novelist Aravind Adiga in his novel *The White Tiger* has captured the possibility of the simmering discontent degenerating into random, uncontrolled and uncontrollable acts of violence. So if only for this consequentialist reason, to prevent outbursts of violence, we need to change our social attitudes and behaviour.

Conservative writers have noted that the game of cricket, which allowed for wealthy landowners and tenant farmers to play together on the village green in England, was simply not something that the French aristocracy would have embraced. The rest as they say is history. The English aristocracy survived and a cohesive English nation went on to achieve much. French aristocrats, barring the ones saved by the Pimpernel, perished at the guillotine. India being India, we may not get the guillotine. But an Adiga-esque picture is not impossible or even improbable.

Conservatives have another reason besides fear to address our social inhumanity. Conservatives believe in the dignity of the individual and are suspicious of the collective. It is therefore morally repugnant that a person be humiliated as a member of the great unwashed collective known as the poor and the weak. He or she must be recognized as an individual, and it is as an individual that he or she needs to be approached, with respect and courtesy.

Obviously, we need processes and systems that nudge us in the direction where our fears are dispelled and our moral uprightness is enhanced. What then in our society is analogous to English village cricket? Do we have mechanisms in our social arena where we do not treat our thin-legged fellow citizens with inhumanity? Frankly, I do not know. What I do know is that this issue has bothered great minds like the Mahatma, who wondered how we could ask for freedom or swaraj when we denied it to so many of our countrymen and countrywomen.

The same issue received considerable attention from our detractors like Kipling who argued that Indians did not deserve freedom principally because we were given to oppressing our women and our poor and in fact it was the British who protected these unhappy residents of our fair land. I leave it to readers to ponder over this problem and think of solutions. I would urge that these be practical social solutions, not tainted by the dead hand of statist intervention that will aggravate rather than resolve the problem.

~

To discuss modern Indian society and not to talk about cricket would be improper and a tad silly. Cricket is the best example of the patent success of not rejecting recent history, of opting for gradual change and not storming the Bastille. Here is a game that started off as a quintessentially English village affair. (We are all aware that the Scots and the Irish have at best a cynical spectator interest in cricket and only one Welsh county, Glamorgan, plays decent cricket.) The British ruled us. Their rule was not always to our liking. They were not that keen to give us the gift of this divine game. But guess what, we took it anyway.

On occasional Saturdays and Sundays when I am in a capacious mood, I conclude that the reason we love cricket is that it is not a game, but a mystic, religious endeavour, and of course Indians love all sacred things. The philosopher Ashis Nandy has gone further when he has spoken ex cathedra, declaring that cricket is actually an Indian game accidentally invented by the English. Cricket has been a unique, unifying cement in our country. The French thinker de Tocqueville would have approved of the fact that this voluntary civic activity has been central to our social cohesion. Roger Scruton would approve of the fact that cricket creates a shared mutuality across otherwise separated social groups. Ram Guha captures this brilliantly when he describes the career of the great cricketer Palwankar Balu, who happened to be a Dalit. Anyone who has watched cricket matches in Indian slums as well as club matches in Shivaji Park,

Saidapet or Basavangudi will understand what I am talking about. Given the sheer size and more recently the increased affluence of the Indian spectator population, almost imperceptibly we have become the most powerful group in international cricketing administration circles. And this has happened even though many illegitimate betting issues emanate in India. In a few centuries, it might be seen as simply an accident that cricket was earlier headquartered in north London. It might end up being seen as one more example of Indian openness and creativity. Of course, in our times it might be as important as our Constitution in unifying us, enthusing us and exciting us.

~

I will deal with Indian films in the section on aesthetics. But I do want to touch just briefly on the social impact of Hindi movies and television serials. The most sensible thing our otherwise silly socialist state did was not to introduce controls and licences on the movie industry. Where the government faced expected resistance in its clumsy attempts to impose Hindi on all states, the Hindi film industry has had greater success through the invisible hand of that civilized institution, the commercial marketplace. This has resulted in what can be described as the Punjabification of the urban Indian middle class in an astonishing manner. In places as far apart as Coimbatore, Guwahati and Vijayawada, no middle-class wedding today can take place without the mehendi and sangeet ceremonies. Almost imperceptibly, without much help but with some attention from the movie industry, the mangalsutra and the sindoor have acquired national footprints.

It has been the case that from the earliest times, both centrifugal and centripetal forces have operated in our society. We are always reviving old commonalities and establishing new ones. To dismiss these changes as market-driven capitalist commodification and intrinsically evil fascist homogenization is to miss the point completely. India is like a multicellular organism where ideas, practices, customs and traditions seep across osmotic porous membranes. That is the way we have always been, and therefore as conservatives we are not unduly perturbed by the so-called homogenization trend, as long as it is gradual, voluntary, organic and not state-driven.

~

Now let us get to the vexed issue of religion in our society. To anyone who is not intentionally obtuse, it must be obvious that to talk about anything Indian without reference to the sacred and the religious is a non-starter. I would argue that we in India are lucky insofar as we are witnesses to religion as a social institution that evolves, rather than one which stays static at the vertex of its single-point origin. This allows us to play the Disraeli trick: we can and we do drop traditions which are not in the stockbroker's buy or hold buckets, but which have clearly reached a sell recommendation.

In the days of the Raj, orientalist scholars felt vindicated by positing the existence of a static Hindu religion which had existed in the same form forever. Subsequent scholarship has demolished this hypothesis. Hinduism, if you must call it a religion, seems to have a chameleon-like adaptability while maintaining a continuous subterranean connect with ancient links. The historian P.V. Kane dates the Vedic Apastamba Sutra to 450 BCE. And this text has a reference to Yuga Dharma, or the virtuous conduct appropriate for the age. With each successive age, gods can disappear, practices can change and social habits can be radically altered. In my own lifetime, I have seen a Punjabi custom known as karva chauth attain national importance, and I have witnessed the complete disappearance of the practice of upper-caste widows shaving their heads. I have witnessed the rise of Sai Baba and Santoshi Ma. Both these cults have elements that cleverly sabotage caste, regional and gender stereotypes.

In 1955 and in 1956, by pushing through the Hindu Marriage Act and the Hindu Succession Act, the self-proclaimed agnostic Jawaharlal Nehru managed to refashion at one stroke the contours that Hindu society had acquired through two and a half centuries of codified colonial formality. We must not forget that Pandit Nehru was only implementing the vision of that brilliant lawgiver Ambedkar. It took an outside scholar like Percival Spear to make the point that with all the obsessions we have with Nehru's economic policies and foreign policy pretensions, we forget that future historians may remember him as an architect of an evolving Hindu society.

~

Other religions in India have demonstrated varying degrees of evolutionary capacity. Buddhism has acquired several interesting characteristics as it has attempted a revival in India in the twentieth century. Today, we are witness to Hinayana–Theravada traditions at Bodh Gaya. These traditions derive encouragement and support from Sri Lanka. Tibetan Buddhism too has gained significance. Easing up of travel to Ladakh and Tawang as well as the presence of Tibetans in places as far away as Karnataka has helped this. The persona of the Dalai Lama, who was forced out of his homeland, has been very important in the reinvigoration process. And of course, Ambedkar's Navayana Buddhism has added tremendous energy in the religious and social spheres. The most recent addition to the Buddhist firmament is the Vipassana movement that has returned long forgotten Indic Buddhist meditation traditions to India via Myanmar. One could argue that Buddhism in India today is somewhat removed from the classical texts like the *Dhammapada* or the *Surangama Sutra*. But that is precisely what religious evolution is all about.

The lively debates and public posturing of the Digambar, Shwetambar and Sthanakvasi Jains constitute another example of religious adaptability and changing contours. Some of them are clamouring for the statutory benefits that accrue to a religious minority. Others remain in a traditional quasi-Hindu state.

The Sikhs have faced greater challenges. The loss of so many hard-won and hard-worked landed assets on account of Partition, and the wounds that this left on this long-suffering religious group have not healed easily. Political chicanery as practised by different political parties has not helped. Nevertheless, a visit to Anandpur Sahib to witness the universality and energy that can be imparted by a talented Israeli architect on this youngest of India's religions remains a heartening phenomenon. The fact remains that Sikhism with its langars, its insistence that even the rich participate in cleaning the gurdwaras and its general emphasis on the dignity of labour is uniquely adapted to the needs of the dharma of the current yuga. I am optimistic that over the next few decades this faith and its adherents will deal with their challenges creatively.

~

Indian Muslims have had to deal for centuries with the foundational debate between Sheikh Sirhindi and Dara Shikoh. Sheikh Sirhindi argued against Akbar's syncretic efforts. He was keen that Indian Muslims not 'contaminate' themselves with Hindu influences, but retain their unalloyed, pure non-Indian identity. The approach of Sirhindi has remained attractive for many who would like to fall back on the puritan orthodoxy of Arabized Islam. Deriving from Dara Shikoh's integrative approach, there arises an attempt to generate an Indian version of the universal Islam, a version that is imbued with Indian peculiarities, eclectic Sufism and even an overlay of the controversial caste system. After Partition, this debate was slowly but steadily getting played out in favour of an eclectic, dialogical option. How can anyone forget that Naushad–Shakeel–Rafi–Dilip gave Hindi films their best bhajans? In the intellectual world, Mushirul Hasan proved that even Uttar Pradesh, which was often considered a Deobandi bastion, had multiple traditions of dialogue and accommodation, a veritable Ganga–Jamuna syncretism.

Nineteen seventy-three changed all that. With the rise in oil prices and the shift in the political centre of the Islamic world from a westernized Egypt to a Wahhabi Saudi Arabia, Indian Islam had to be affected. This change is not unique to India. Its impact has been felt in places as unlikely as the mosques of London, Paris, Hamburg, Toronto, Jakarta and Penang. Usage of the veil was gradually diminishing in the 1950s and 1960s. That has been reversed. Muslim institutions are under financial and psychological pressure to become more rigid and to downplay syncretic trends. There is a silver lining though, as fortunately the Sufi school seems to be acquiring fresh energy. This is particularly true in the field of music.

I would argue that Islam in India has the best opportunity of providing creative and, may I add with some trepidation, evolutionary responses to contemporary challenges. The rise of Muslim mahila organizations, the new energy among Pasmanda Muslims, who are embracing their pre-conversion caste identities, ironically with an eye on the goodies conferred on backward castes, are interesting new developments that need to be watched carefully. The scale that India provides by its sheer size has ensured that despite numerous hurdles, brilliant individual Muslims continue to make their mark in many fields. The Premjis, the Khorakiwalas, the Hamieds in business have demonstrated that a neutral market rewards risk-takers impartially. The strong Muslim presence in Bollywood suggests that Indian audiences respond to talent without any prejudice. It is particularly heartening to note that Muslim actors are no longer under pressure to change their screen names. There are no Dilip Kumars and Meena Kumaris today.

The publication of the Sachar Committee Report showed that the claims of the socialist rulers of being sensitive 'caretakers' of Muslims were completely bogus. Some of my Muslim friends were surprised that the worst performer was Marxist-ruled West Bengal. But as I pointed out to them, what else could one expect from these immoral apparatchiks? One good effect of the Sachar Report has been that middle-class Muslims have figured out that they have to assign greater agency to themselves and take up more voluntary educational activities instead of concentrating resources on lavish well-lit mosques. This tradition was already strong in south India and is now gathering momentum elsewhere.

Conservatives need to laud individuals as individuals, outside of limited identities. That there is a vigorous attempt to reform Muslim personal laws, an attempt that is admittedly sixty years after the 1955 and 1956 Hindu reforms, has to be a source of optimism. Those who want to push through these changes with haste tend to want to do so for political reasons. The conservative position has to be that gradual change combining legislation, judicial verdicts and community consensus is the correct option to root for.

Issues connected with Indian Muslims that do not deal with religion are largely seen through a political prism and not a social one. I believe that this is a mistake. Muslims are more than just voters. They have given to the country important legacies in architecture, painting, music, dress, food, landscape gardening, literature and much more. To view them only through the political lens and, worse, to encourage them to view themselves in this manner is a travesty that we must avoid.

We must keep rooting for a creative Indian Islam, even if the global situation right now seems inimical to this idea. It is perhaps politically incorrect to say so, but I have a feeling that Naipaul got it right: Indonesia and India are two countries where Islamic intellectual discourse might free itself from puritan Arab imperialism. Naipaul had an indifferent opinion of Rushdie, whom he thought of as a minor writer. But in a few decades or even centuries, we may conclude that Rushdie, just precisely by stoking extreme fatwa responses, may have ensured the start of a long path of recrimination, introspection and an eventual renaissance. A person might emerge who ends up as a combination of Dara Shikoh, the Sufis Amir Khusro and Sarmad and the modernist Syed Ahmad Khan, and he or she might be someone who revitalizes the Islamic intellect. This might end up being Indian Islam's most important contribution to the world. That the writer Javed Akhtar, though born a Muslim, is willing to proclaim his atheism suggests that within India, with its freedoms, however limited, a vigorous intellectual discourse can and will arise and hopefully this will prove creative.

Sufficient attention has not been given to writers in Tamil and Malayalam, who only incidentally happen to be Muslim. The earliest writings by Muslims in Tamil go back some nine hundred years. Today, there is even a vigorous school of Muslim feminist writing in Tamil. The well-known Rajathi Salma has become an exemplar for this school. Needless to say, these represent attempts to explore new territories and need to be encouraged because they are filled with so much promise.

~

The Syrian Christian Church in India is an ancient one, having both a Nestorian and an Orthodox component. With the coming of the Portuguese, some opted for communion with Rome while retaining their Syriac liturgy. With the coming of the British, some may have seen material rather than spiritual advantages in sharing a communion with the Anglicans. In any event, there are today half a dozen schismatic branches of the original church purportedly founded by the apostle St Thomas. Over the centuries, Syrian Christians have successfully navigated within the interstices of India's caste system. They have continued to demonstrate an interesting adaptive and evolutionary capability as they deal with Kerala's fractious democratic politics. Theirs has been a focus on the practical. They have not thrown up any significant theologian or philosopher. But they have produced many successful politicians, businesspersons, scientists, artists, writers and bureaucrats. They have also provided considerable excitement to their adherents and the Kerala press, by their penchant for theatrical quarrels in the public sphere as for example when one group forcibly occupies a property controlled by another group.

The Roman Catholic Church in India has demonstrated originality and energy. Francis Xavier represented a controversial ecstatic and proselytizing side of the Jesuit order. Roberto de Nobili and Father Stephens, both Jesuits, one Italian and the other English, were able to imaginatively engage with Indic traditions and religions, one in Tamil Nadu and one in Maharashtra. In the twentieth century, another Jesuit, Father Antony de Mello, revived this tradition. He combined mysticism with eclecticism. For some time, the church establishment persecuted de Mello, tried to silence him and even threatened him with excommunication. He held his ground. His respectful, sensitive and erudite engagement with Hinduism, Sufism and Buddhism has resulted in a truly original contribution to religious philosophy, which is deeply Indian.

Interesting personalities like the political leader Rajkumari Amrit Kaur, the Gandhian economist J.C. Kumarappa and the husband and wife team of Violet and Joachim Alva, as well as Jaipal Singh from Jharkhand, made a significant impact on the national movement. They successfully countered the preferred British position that Indian Christians were supporters of British rule, without any reservations – something that the self-styled All India Christian Association eagerly demonstrated. This association enthusiastically funded Jinnah, arguing that Christians would be better off under a monotheistic Islamic dispensation than in a country where the majority were polytheistic idolaters. Needless to say, time has proved this contention as being completely misguided and erroneous. Christians in India have fared very well in all fields, while tragically, in Pakistan, they are hounded and persecuted.

Mainstream Protestant denominations have preferred to remain pro-establishment, depending on whichever establishment is in place at any given point in time. They have established a working arrangement with the Indian environment, which is both practical and matter-of-fact. They have focused on education, including education of the lower castes, without causing too many ripples. The one exception to this has been the Baptist church in the north-east. The Reverend Michael Scott seems to have abused the trust placed in him by the Indian government, to encourage Naga irredentism. This has damaged Christian missionaries elsewhere in India, who now have to keep answering questions about whether they are subversive apropos of their activities in tribal areas.

In the last three decades, there has been a tremendous increase in the activities of charismatic evangelicals and Pentecostals who draw inspiration and funding from church groups in the American South, from states like Texas and Oklahoma. They represent a specific discontinuity from the traditions of adjustment so characteristic of the Syrian churches. Armed with the conviction that worship of multiple deities and idols is satanic, and being willing to say so in public and in printed documents, these groups challenge existing social arrangements. They cannot be treated like other Christian denominations, principally because they do not wish to be. They aggressively challenge the status quo in large parts of rural and small-town India. Among other things, India faces a quizzical foreign policy challenge. These churches receive financial and moral support from US citizens, who also constitute the base of the Republican Party. Confronting their extreme behaviour on the ground may end up alienating key political constituencies in a country whose friendship we want. How Indian society and the Indian state approach this challenge will be interesting to watch.

We should not forget that a hundred years ago it was common for Christian missionaries to denigrate Rama, Krishna and Allah in public marketplaces in Indian small towns. Today, however, we see that mainstream churches in India have consciously incorporated diyas, garlands, Indian classical music and even Bharatanatyam into their rituals. Over time, as the air of India mellows evangelicals and Pentecostals, perhaps they too will reach a uniquely Indian accommodation.

~

The Zoroastrians in India are in a downward demographic spiral. Their extraordinary achievements in diverse fields over the last two centuries now seem headed for the museum along with Chaldeans and Incas. The fundamental problem is the inability of sections of their leadership to give up a patriarchal mindset, which effectively limits the number of children of mixed marriages that they can absorb. Their ancient and solemn commitment supposedly made to a king in coastal Gujarat, that they would not proselytize and convert, has now come back to bite them badly. It seems unlikely that they will extricate themselves from the cul-de-sac that they are trapped in. Sometimes, I feel glad in a bittersweet way that at least my generation has known so many Parsis and that their final confrontation with history will happen after I am gone. Unfortunately, most of our children may have to live in an India without Parsis, a sadder and poorer India. The new Jiyo Parsi movement may yet ensure that my pessimistic prognosis does not prevail. I raise a toast to that prospect.

The Jews in India have made substantial contributions to our country.

Garcia de Orta, in the sixteenth century, pioneered studies in Indian botany and pharmacology. It appears that de Orta formally converted to Catholicism to evade the attentions of the Portuguese Inquisition. But the Inquisition fathers were not easily fooled. After de Orta's death, they 'proved' that he was a secret Jew and exhumed his grave. De Orta seems to have had friends and acquaintances among the residents of Maratha territories around the then Portuguese Bombay. Of course, some of these contacts would have been Bene Israels, who faced no persecution or Inquisition in Maratha territory.

Modern Indian art criticism cannot be thought of without Rudolf von Leyden and Walther Langhammer. Although they were migrants fleeing persecution in Europe, von Lyden and Langhammer were Indian in virtually every way. Nissim Ezekiel, incidentally a political conservative, is central to modern Indian poetry. General J.F.R. Jacob was a key planner in the 1971 war. Leela Samson has been an important contributor to the development of the Bharatanatyam dance form.

Indian Jews have traditionally taken pride in the fact that India is probably the only country in the world where they have not faced persecution, excluding the horrors perpetrated by the Portuguese Inquisition in Goa. Indian Jews had almost disappeared as the Bene Israel, the Cochin Jews and the Baghdadis migrated in large numbers to the Promised Land of Israel. All of a sudden, new Jewish communities have been discovered, if that is the right word, in places as far off as the north-east and Andhra Pradesh. This, combined with India's growing relationship with Israel and the large number of young Israeli tourists we host, might yet result in a revival of Jewish presence in India. Again, as is to be expected from this people, their contributions are likely to be vastly disproportionate to their numbers.

The Bahais, who are relentlessly persecuted in Iran, the land of their birth, are demonstrating amazing energy and creativity in fields as diverse as architecture and law. This religion, which is clearly in tune with the dharma of the current yuga, has given us a gorgeous architectural masterpiece in its Lotus Temple in Delhi.

~

Net, net, conservatives need to feel good about the current state of Indian society. Many practices that assault the dignity of the individual still remain. But gradual, systematic changes in the caste system, in gender relations and the emergence of solidarity across caste groups are happening on the ground. The Hindutva movement may be one of the factors behind this phenomenon. At one level, the Hindutva movement attempts to create a pan-Hindu identity that transcends caste. At another level, the movement encourages hitherto 'neglected' castes like Pasis and Rajbongshis to assert proud identities. At a third symbolic level, the Hindutva movement gives Dalits public pride of place in activities like laying the foundation stones of temples. At a fourth substantive level, more and more of their leaders, including their present most important leader, Narendra Modi, are brought in from outside the traditional dominant castes. All these actions, irrespective of the political motives behind them, do encourage a level of solidarity and the emergence of a 'band of brothers' across caste barriers.

Our religious traditions are also coping with change, with the uniquely Indian characteristics of adaptability when faced with the challenging demands of the times. And I say all of this despite the current concerns on the part of many that we are descending into a mighty abyss of intolerance on account of the politics associated with castes and religions. But considering social and societal aspects, and for the moment keeping politics aside, I feel bold enough to state the case for being modestly sanguine, which of course is the best that conservatives hope for.

Additionally, many of our evolutionary social changes are happening organically rather than through clumsy state intervention. In many cases, the state discovers facts like increased intercaste or interregional marriages, new and adaptive religious movements, unintended consequences of voluntary migrations and so many other phenomena, after they have happened. We must thank God for small mercies. If the state had discovered these matters earlier, dysfunctional interference would have followed to the detriment of the organic features of our society.

5

Aesthetics and Education

Now to the last of our subjects, aesthetics – and a subject which, as I explain later, is closely impacted by aesthetics – education.

It all started with orientalism. Let me state the basic orientalist premises. Indian sculpture lacked classical simplicity. It was too ornate, confused and bordering on the grotesque. The only partially sophisticated Indian sculpture was on account of Greek influence on the Gandhara school. Indian painting lacked an understanding of perspective and was therefore childish. Indian music lacked harmony and therefore could not be considered an evolved art. There was nothing in Indian drama comparable to the Periclean or the Elizabethan stages. Because it was sculptural in its tone, Hindu,

Buddhist and Jain architecture was unimpressive. The only Indian architecture worth talking about was the Islamic school. There, too, ornate schools like the Gujarati Muslim school of architecture needed to be at a discount. Indian literature was almost exclusively focused on religion and myths. It was as if it had never come of age. India lacked any sound aesthetic theory. Art remained at best at the folk level. Indian crafts, as distinct from art, in the form of its textiles, brass, bronzes, carpets and furniture had a childlike and primitive charm. But none of these could stand up to solid aesthetic standards.

In fairness, side by side with this hypercritical orientalism, there was a school of British thinkers led by William Jones, and which included James Prinsep, Alexander Cunningham, Robert Sewell, G.V. Pope and Edwin Arnold, that oscillated between a balanced, sober affection for Indian culture and occasionally an enthusiasm which was a tad excessive.

Over the years, the extreme condescending orientalist positions have been pretty much demolished. A tradition of aesthetic scholarship going back to the legendary Bharata Muni, to Sarangadeva, to Abhinavagupta, to Appayya Dikshita, to Jagannatha Pandita and many others existed in our country. The Navarasa theory, which posits that the aesthetic experience emanates from the rise and fall of nine emotive states, has retained its originality and its relevance, and today seems to fit in with some of the insights of neuroscience. The texts of the *Natya Shastra* and *Shilpa Shastra* traditions continue to be mined for insights that are timeless and refreshing.

And while conquests and destruction did lead to some discontinuities, there remained a flowing stream within the tradition. For example, even as there was what our erstwhile rulers liked to call pre-British anarchy in the land, Tanjore maintained and enhanced artistic traditions right from the Chola period of the tenth–eleventh centuries through the Nayaka and Maratha periods from the sixteenth to the nineteenth centuries. And isolated Himalayan kingdoms, such as in Ladakh, Kashmir, Chamba and Spiti, produced astonishingly important and beautiful art from the tenth century onward right through till the early twentieth century.

Another kind of subterranean continuity also operated. *Kakanakote,* by Maasti, the great twentieth-century Kannada writer, can be seen as deriving its inspiration from Kalidasa's classic *Abhijnanashakuntalam.* They both deal with the theme of an urban sophisticate marrying a nature nymph, represented by a maiden from the forests. For that matter, when in the seventeenth century a Nayaka king wrote a dance drama depicting the divine wedding of Senkamala Nachiar to Rajagopalaswamy, he was deriving his content and his technique from another monarch, the sixteenth-century Vijayanagara emperor Krishna Deva Raya, who wrote the graceful *Amukta Malyada*. The tradition of kings writing plays and composing music that their subjects admired goes back to Mahendra Varma Pallava in the seventh century and comes down all the way to Wajid Ali Shah in the nineteenth century, whose compositions and choreographies around Lord Krishna were loved by his subjects.

Despite the attempts at suffocation on the part of orientalist British administrators and puritanical Christian missionaries, Indian art of all kinds – the classical, the folk, the pan-Indian and the regional – not only did not die, but it demonstrated an astonishing vitality. In fact, British rule and colonial disdain might have given us an added incentive to light the fires of our creativity. At least until now we have not had to face the poignant pain of Roger Scruton and his friends, as English church music seems to be disappearing.

We have produced scholars of aesthetics. Vishnu Narayan Bhatkande, Ananda Coomaraswamy and the extraordinary multifaceted genius Rabindranath Tagore stand out as significant art historians and philosophical minds. Fortunately, not all foreign scholars were of the patronizing variety. Stella Kramrisch and Heinrich Zimmer made significant positive contributions to the study of Indian art.

With the coming of Independence, the country found a new pride and new energy in its art scene. It was not just painting, sculpture, music, dance and drama that flourished. Aesthetics as a branch of philosophy and as a close cousin of political philosophy also got its fair share of attention. Kamaladevi Chattopadhyaya, B.N. Goswami, Sivaramamurti, K.K. Nair who wrote under the pseudonym of Krishna Chaitanya and others were joined by brilliant and sympathetic foreigners like Anna Dallapiccola, David Shulman, George Michell and Richard Blurton in this endeavour.

Conservatives have every reason to be happy about the current state of both highbrow and popular art in India. We have not abandoned traditions and sought refuge in sterile modernism or that abomination, postmodernism. If anything, declining folk and other traditions have been revived and the disdain for so-called folk art has disappeared. It has become fashionable to talk of India's soft power. If such a thing exists, it is because despite all the glitzy influences of technology, we have kept faith in our unique artistic traditions, our diversities and our connections with the sacred.

～

The Indian movie industry is an excellent example of India's aesthetic success. The first movie to be made in India was *Raja Harishchandra*, over a hundred years ago. Of course, one can dismiss this as an upper-caste Hindu response to Western assaults. The director of *Raja Harishchandra*, Dadasaheb Phalke, was an enormously sensitive person who in hostile times managed to demonstrate that the gupta nadi or subterranean stream of our culture has been running from antiquity. The enduring success of mythological themes and bhakti tales in our cinematic world may appear unsophisticated to movie critics; they may appear as hegemonic power plays to the followers of Foucault. But conservatives see in them a healthy continuation of melas, jatras, lavani, kathakali, yakshagana, araiyar sevai, temple dancing, teru-koottu and so on. Their very range, from the folksy to the ritualistic, gives them the strength of the common people. Burke complimented the judgements of the uneducated 'swain' who possessed innate conservative good sense. M.K. Thyagaraja Bhagavatar playing Bhakti saints, N.T. Rama Rao playing Rama and Krishna, M.S. Subbulakshmi playing Meera, Sandhya playing Shakuntala, Bharat Bhushan playing Baiju Bawra and Dilip Kumar playing a modern version of Ram and Shyam, all stand out for their popularity which snooty folks may find not acceptable, but which tell you that Indian film from its origins remained pretty strongly Indian. And it was not restricted to Hindu themes. *Chaudhvin Ka Chand* and *Mere Mehboob* could have been produced and could have succeeded only in India. They would have been out of place in Egypt or Turkey.

To talk of Indian popular art and not pay attention to the garish colours, extravagant songs, vibrant dances, histrionic and unrealistic dialogues and hackneyed stories of Indian movies is like talking of British culture and ignoring music halls and Gilbert and Sullivan, not to mention *Eastenders* and *Monty Python*. I have always felt that there was an inexorable cinematic necessity to script 'Roop Tera Mastaana', 'Choli Ke Peechhey', 'Rang Barsey', 'Aaj Phir Jeeney Ki Tamanna', 'Maanasa Myne Varu', 'Kanna Moochee' and 'Chhaiyan Chhaiyan' exactly the way they were.

Given India's diversity, our film industry has managed to combine the highbrow with the popular in virtually every region and language. Bengal gave us Satyajit Ray, Ritwik Ghatak and Mrinal Sen. Jayakanthan made only one movie, *Unnaipol Oruvan* – a commercial flop and an undoubted classic. Guru Dutt has over the years emerged as a cult figure in world cinema. Satyadev Dubey's Marathi classic *Shantata Court Chalu Ahe* has stood the test of time. Amol Palekar's contributions are worth watching while lying on a couch in a pensive mood.

The Kannada classics *Samskara, Vamsha Vriksha, Taayi Saheba* and *Chomana Dudi*, among others, stand out if for no other reason than their universalist patina, even as they are deeply embedded in the Kannada land. Shyam Benegal has a wide repertoire that never seems to fade away. The list can go on and on. The fact that stands out is how rooted they all are in India and Indian culture. Whether highbrow or popular, you can never mistake an Indian movie for anything other than it being Indian.

In other countries, the relationship between movies and music is not as deep as it is in India. We have developed a whole genre known as film music. Our film music directors, lyricists and playback singers may constitute our own unique contribution to world culture in the twentieth and twenty-first centuries. Our music directors in particular have been the finest synthesizers of various diversities. They have borrowed freely from Indian classical ragas and Indian folk music. Naushad, Salil Chowdhury, S.D. Burman, Madan Mohan, Roshan, Khayyam, Bhupen Hazarika and Viswanathan–Ramamurthy come to mind. They have also created aural delights for their audiences by bringing in musical themes and traditions from around the world, for example, R.D. Burman, Laxmikant–Pyarelal, Ilayaraaja and A.R. Rahman. But of course, these are shorthand lists at best. The list of brilliant creators of music in the Indian film industry simply goes on and on. And the singers they composed for – be it Lata, Asha or Manna Dey, Hemant Kumar, Mukesh, Talat or Rafi, Sushila, Srinivas or Balasubrahmanyam – they never let them down.

We are today a country where men and women in every corner are humming and singing film tunes and songs from dawn to dusk. Film music arguably has entered our bloodstreams and our neural synapses. I hate to be repetitive. But the point needs to be made. Film music, particularly with the extensive use of playback singers, has emerged as something uniquely Indian and is one more proof of the fact that the idea of India remains very much alive. It is not a reactionary conceit. It just happens to rise up from the soil and the stubble of our land.

~

The only areas where we face disappointment are where there has been the usual incompetent state intervention. The Sahitya Akademi, the Lalit Kala Akademi and the Sangeet Natak Akademi have wasted taxpayer money funding inane and banal activities. Of course, this is in addition to their orthographic incompetence. But even in this sphere, there have been exceptions. It was the active intervention of All India Radio that gave new life to classical music. In central India, Bharat Bhavan and the Museum of Tribal Art, both government projects, have produced architectural gems and creative spaces of considerable vibrancy. Institutions like Bharat Bhavan almost always go through ups and downs. In this context, it is heartening to see the emergence of classy imitators, like the Jawahar Kala Kendra in Jaipur. Government sponsorship of the Festival of India and its conduct by the brilliant art historian Pupul Jayakar started off as an effort to showcase India to the world. It ended up becoming an extraordinary vehicle for encouraging our traditional arts, crafts and performing traditions. They have all acquired fresh energy and are seamlessly embedded in contemporary India.

~

All India Radio deserves credit for supporting both Hindustani and Carnatic classical music. But the real credit for the vigour and gusto of these art forms in recent times goes to the artistes themselves. Ravi Shankar made Indian classical music part of the world scene. M.S. Subbulakshmi created a new edition of the musical *Mother India*. Bhimsen Joshi and Balamurali Krishna took vocal renditions into enchanting territories, even as Kishori Amonkar redefined the meaning of the Sanskrit word 'kokila'. Bismillah Khan, Hariprasad Chaurasia,

Lalgudi Jayaraman, Vilayat Khan and Amjad Ali Khan expanded the realms of instrumental music, again leading them past new and exquisite thresholds. The list can go on. Suffice it to say that there is no dearth of energy, talent or achievement in Indian classical music, and its future looks assured.

~

Modern Indian achievements in the aesthetic sphere have happened largely despite the deadening hand of the state, primarily on account of the creativity, energy and exuberance of our human capital and the ability of both our practitioners and our audiences to leverage our association with our inherited traditions. Our aesthetic sensibility is inextricably tied to our education system and one might have hoped that we would do well in our educational efforts. However, this sanguine prospect has not prevailed. The devaluing of the liberal arts and humanities in our educational system has, to a great extent, resulted in recent generations being ignorant of our own aesthetic traditions, and it has stifled the development of aesthetic sensibilities among modern urban planners, architects and, indeed, the populace in general. Let us proceed to examine this rather painful subject.

Education was both a failure and a success in the days of the Raj. The country was left largely illiterate, and this was during the rule of the British, who were definitely aware that England had crossed 50 per cent literacy levels in Elizabethan times. They were also aware of the educational reforms in Maria Theresa's Austria, nineteenth-century Prussia and Meiji Japan.

The failures of our British rulers were compounded by our own. Even in 1947, there were more Christian missionary schools in India than schools set up by private Indian individuals or societies. Ramaswamy Naicker made the poignant comment that if we spent on education a fraction of what we spent on religious rituals, we would be so much better off. Maraimalai Adigal made the same observation. The best attempts of the Ramakrishna Mission, the Arya Samaj, the Theosophical Society and the Servants of India Society remained woefully inadequate. Our maharajas, with the honourable exceptions of the rulers of Mysore, Baroda, Travancore and Cochin, were a darned sight worse than our foreign rulers. They had money for palaces, jewels, cars and polo. But educating their subjects was a low priority matter. Literacy rates in the princely states were a fraction of the abysmally low rates in British India.

Higher education, curiously enough, got a better deal. In the mid-nineteenth century, the universities of Bombay, Calcutta and Madras were established. The English historian Correlli Barnett makes the case that the focus of the British was on academic subjects with great emphasis on English literature and law, with insufficient attention given to the sciences and engineering. Nevertheless, several colleges focused on engineering, medicine, agriculture, mining and forestry were set up in India. J.N. Tata and the Maharaja of Mysore set up the Indian Institute of Science. Madan Mohan Malaviya built on Annie Besant's efforts to set up the Banaras Hindu University. Syed Ahmad Khan set up the college which became the Aligarh Muslim University. Rabindranath Tagore established the Visva-Bharati University at Santiniketan in rural Bengal. Net, net, India emerged fairly strong in higher education once we attained Independence.

The more things change, the more they remain the same is something that the French are accustomed to saying. And occasionally, the French are right in what they say. At least insofar as Indian education is concerned, the French have it right all the way. Despite all the rhetoric of egalitarianism and faux socialism, the governments in free India, both in Delhi and in the state capitals, neglected school education and literacy while spending, and on occasion wasting, money on higher education. Even in a relatively well-governed state like Tamil Nadu, there was no free school education till the mid-1960s. Believe it or not, government-aided schools charged fees till then, effectively giving the message that it was completely appropriate for the children of the poorest in our country to stay illiterate. This is despite the fact that the so-called wicked Indian capitalists even as early as the 1940s, in their famous Bombay Plan, had called for free primary, secondary, tertiary and vocational education.

As always, it is the socialist clique that had run our country for so many decades after Independence that once more showed its anti-poor credentials. The American political scientist Myron Weiner has made the case that this reflected Indian upper-class and upper-caste insensitivity, which we have discussed earlier. According to him, it was also derived from fears that literacy would destroy a flourishing labour market of low-wage workers and that the literate may become socially assertive a la Charles Dickens's character the Marquis de St Evermonde, from *A Tale of Two Cities*, who wants to keep the common people suppressed.

The net result is that many decades have gone by since South Korea attained hundred per cent literacy and we are still not there. The problem is that ill-developed human capital results in reducing economic growth prospects. It is also obscene not to have fellow citizens whose capacities are developed. And if we did not already know it, Amartya Sen has reminded us of this. It was the Vajpayee government which finally decided that sarva shiksha or education for everyone should be a minimum national commitment. The physical numbers in terms of schools and classrooms have been put in place. Quality and content are still at a discount. Progress is slow, but it is discernible. Not good enough, but that is what we have.

Considerable attention and resources were devoted to higher education in the early years of independent India. Our omniscient Planning Commission wanted us to imitate the great Soviet Union and produce steel and machines. Institutes of technology, medical sciences and management were pampered with vast quantities of land and money. They were encouraged to collaborate with foreign experts, and very soon India was producing a reasonably large number of these qualified professionals.

The irony was that our brilliantly planned economy kept growing at a snail's pace and the high quality human capital just could not be absorbed in India. This coincided with the liberalization of immigration quotas in countries like the US and Canada. Qualified Indian professionals have flocked not only to North America, but also to Britain, to the oil-rich Middle East, to Singapore and elsewhere. There is hardly a country in the world where we will not today find Indian engineers, managers, academics, scientists, accountants, doctors and nurses. The abjectly poor Indian taxpayers have amply funded the human capital of rich countries. I once met a foreigner who was mighty impressed by how highly educated all Indians were. I had to explain to him that all the Indians he had met were well educated but that somehow, somewhere, we had forgotten several hundred millions left behind in India who could not even read and write. He thought that I was a strange kind of liar.

Never mind, even silly state actions can have unintended consequences. The Indian diaspora has emerged as a national strength. The corridor connecting Bengaluru to San Jose and Silicon Valley and other similar corridors are giving us economic benefits. At least some parts of our brain drain have been converted into a brain bank.

Being a 'developing country' at a time when development economics has been fashionable, we did develop a level of intellectual achievement in economics. Being a complex, diverse country with multiple kinds of social organizations, we have a great laboratory for sociologists to gorge themselves. While the great sociologist Ghurye straddled two time periods, before and after Independence, free India saw the emergence of reasonably classy scholarship in the social sciences, even if all actors were not of a conservative bent of mind. M.N. Srinivas, Dharma Kumar, T.N. Madan and André Béteille come to mind. But this was not to last. A gradual coarsening of our intellectual fabric occurred, which paralleled the takeover of academia in the West by Marxists and postmodernists. This was in part accentuated in India on account of what appears to be a conscious plan. The Paris protests of 1968 perhaps gave Indira Gandhi a fright. As part of her strategy to tame and house-train possibly difficult leftists, she set up several institutions where these groupies could be safely kept away as members of pointless debating societies. The unintended consequence of this action is that there are numerous places all over the country where the cockamamie meanderings of the European and American left have gained popularity and even a certain kind of hegemony.

As I have mentioned earlier, these academic establishments have been a really bad influence on intellectual discourse in our country. From up in the sky, Indira Gandhi might argue that this is a small price to pay in order to bribe these folks and bottle them up so that they do not cause any harm in the real world. Unfortunately, she forgot that ideas have consequences. The dim-witted discourse that today often gets passed off as legitimate scholarship continues to impose severe costs and much harm in our struggling country. Defeating the chatterati and the priviligentsia, as the journalist Shekhar Gupta calls them, will not be an easy task. But this task can on no account be shirked. It must be undertaken with intrepidity and determination.

At the end of seventy years, all sectors of Indian education have reached a sorry state. We have done somewhat well in setting up schools. But our unionized teachers simply do not bother to come to work and when they do, they do not usually bother to teach. We are running the risk of children attending school but learning next to nothing. It is not a secret that most of these unionized teachers send their own children to private schools.

Meanwhile, we strangle private schools with quixotic laws, like the Right to Education Act. The Centre for Civil Society has demonstrated that parents are happier and learning outcomes are better in private schools where teachers are paid less than the unionized education aristocracy in government schools, and where the returns to expenditure demonstrate significantly higher levels of efficiency than that found in government schools. Apart from being inefficient and costly institutions primarily run not for the benefit of children but for the benefit of the education bureaucracy, our government schools are also being forced to crucify themselves on the cross of linguistic chauvinism.

One need not go into the reasons. The plain facts are as follows: parents of Indian children want their children to go to English-medium schools; government officials send their own children to English-medium schools;

our politicians will not hear of anything but an English-medium school for their children. Yet day in and day out, in state after state, committees of experts keep insisting that the democratic aspirations of parents be put aside, the hypocritical private behaviour of the experts themselves be ignored, and the children of the poor be forced to study in a medium of instruction that they do not want. No wonder in state after state, government schools are emptying out.

The only way out is to push for a voucher system where the state provides parents with vouchers, which they then 'pay' to the schools that they, and not some bureaucrat, choose. As conservatives, we must keep hammering away on this subject. I have of late started making the argument that vouchers will be vote-winners, election-winners. It is an uphill task. There are many vested interests, including teachers' unions, and these unions gain added strength from the fact that the Election Commission uses them as polling officials during elections, and that is a very crucial role. As a result, politicians are reluctant to take on these unions. Despite these obstacles, the fight for respecting the choices of parents must go on.

The higher education crisis is even more spectacular. Not only are the best Indian minds engaged with molecular biology or modern algebra or structural engineering or genetic oncology working in foreign countries, of late we seem to have even outsourced to foreign universities new research in Telugu literature, the Navarasa paradigm or Sanskrit textual analysis. This is true even of Gandhian studies. While Tridib Suhrud and Rajni Bakshi heroically plod on in India, brilliant Gandhian scholars like Anthony Parel and Rajmohan Gandhi have been forced to seek foreign pastures.

In the 1850s the then governor general Lord Dalhousie wrote a note or a minute, suggesting that Indian universities should confine themselves to prescribing syllabi, conducting examinations and awarding degrees. In his view, the creation of new knowledge was best left to Oxford, Cambridge, Glasgow and Edinburgh. We have lived up faithfully to Dalhousie's notions. We are complacently sitting back and watching all research and the creation of new knowledge happen beyond our borders, even when such work is undertaken by Indians. We risk remaining a nation of imitators. In the last twenty years, Indian students have become one of the most important fee revenue sources for American, British and Australian universities. I guess we can feel happy that we are globalizing ourselves. But to globalize from a position of domestic weakness is hardly something worth commending.

In recent times, the Indian state seems to have woken up to the fact that our universities should be freed from bureaucratic octopuses, like the University Grants Commission, that institutions of excellence should be encouraged and that private universities should be allowed. Mind you, it is still very difficult for private individuals or groups to set up universities. It is ironic that under foreign rulers, Besant, Malaviya, Sir Syed and Tagore had it easier. The damage that has been done will take some time to undo. But I am optimistic that in twenty years, we will have a Nobel laureate teaching and researching in India, and that thousands of foreigners will flock to India to obtain PhDs. The legacy of the damage is so deep that I do not think we can crunch that time frame.

Some have argued that private universities can fill this space. I would beg to differ. Even in countries like the US, where there are many private universities, a strong public university system exists as a foundational element. While some private universities can and will do well, others will end up being venal degree factories. We cannot and must not give up on the task of having an excellent public university system.

～

A sympathetic foreigner has written somewhere that although Indians are nice and friendly people, they live in the dirtiest country in the world. For a people with such a strong sense of colours and patterns, which govern our visual aesthetic, our utter indifference to the filth all around us remains a horrifying puzzle. Most of our small towns have no sewage systems and manage with unsightly open drains. On both sides of every highway and railway track we dump plastic and other solid waste, which seems to accumulate forever. Our major rivers are turning into filthy drains and our minor streams and nullahs have become fetid. We seem to leave construction debris anywhere and everywhere that we choose to. Despite a few honourable exceptions, our temples are filthy and off-putting. Our cities have become homes to numerous stray dogs; some have become feral, routinely attacking and killing children. Mosquito-borne diseases, which are on the decline elsewhere, are on the rise in India. It seems inconceivable, but it is true that Indians are dying in large numbers of dengue and malaria and gastrointestinal diseases. Our insanitary conditions have resulted in the resurgence of a once disappearing disease, tuberculosis. We are the TB capital of the world. Our government proudly announced the end of leprosy. Now we know that our government lied. This dreadful disease still persists, and ending government funding may actually lead to an increase in its prevalence.

For decades, our socialist state, with a cosy elite ensconced in Delhi, simply ignored the realities of the country. It has taken a nationalist government to emphasize the importance of a Clean India or a Swachh Bharat. This government has also focused on trying to end open defecation. However, mere state action is likely to prove inadequate. We need to see this as a social and cultural problem where citizens have to be part of the solution. The fact of the matter is that countries with similar levels of poverty are cleaner than India. A visit to clean Sri Lanka ends up providing literally a breath of fresh air.

It is important that the responsibility for improving the present state of affairs be accepted by citizens who have both rights and responsibilities and who are not simply objects of a nanny state. This is one area where I believe voluntary actions by civic groups, so prized by conservatives, have an important role to play. Even modest success in this realm will make our country a cleaner, nicer, safer, prettier place to live in.

We should not lose hope that this cannot be done. We have ample evidence of private sector success and state sector failure. In our cities and towns, the new shopping malls are clean and many actually have clean toilets. As soon as we step out of these malls, we find streets with potholes, with construction debris everywhere, with plastic strewn all over the place and stray dogs on the prowl. There simply is no good reason why public spaces cannot be as clean as the malls. We must take back from the state this vital area, where its dead hand is suffocating us.

~

For a country which has built the Sanchi stupa, the Tanjore temple, the Gol Gumbaz and the Taj Mahal, we have today much to be ashamed of. Despite having many talented architects like Charles Correa and B.V. Doshi, our governments have let us down in the realm of public architecture. Sterile Chandigarh designed by an arrogant totalitarian, an underwhelming Gandhinagar, a dishevelled Navi Mumbai and a half-empty Naya Raipur stand out as cities that we need to be worried about. Luckily, Bhubaneswar has some charming and somewhat heartening features. The public sector creations of Bhilai, Bokaro and Neyveli are soulless tributes to the benevolence of the murderous Comrade Stalin. Luckily, traditional Indian litter and disorganization have somewhat humanized these settlements, as one can hardly call them towns or cities. One hopes that we do better with Amaravati. But I certainly have some trepidation on that count.

The ghastly PWD architecture all over the country, including in our overindulgent capital city, is another sad commentary on the state of affairs. Private sector architecture too has been pretty disappointing as more and more of it tries to imitate the glass and steel structures of a shiny Singapore. The only small silver lining one can see is a renewed focus on restoring old buildings. The desperate determination to neglect the Raj legacy seems to have finally been left behind.

~

From architecture and town planning, I would like to move on to issues connected with ecology and the environment, viewing them through the prisms of aesthetics and conservative philosophy. The legal concept of trusteeship goes back to the King's Chancery courts of medieval England. The idea that a trustee holds property for the benefit of others and that she has a fiduciary responsibility to husband the assets embedded in the trust is an English common law concept which does not exist in continental codes like the Code Napoleon. India too has a hoary tradition of trusteeship. There are innumerable inscriptions on temple walls where kings, merchants, artisans and even courtesans have donated land to be held in trust for the deity within the temple. In addition, they have dug wells, built reservoirs and erected dharamshalas and endowed them for the benefit of future generations of pilgrims and commoners. In Gujarat and Rajasthan, we have examples of numerous stepwells set up for similar purposes by chieftains and merchants, going back several centuries. The famous Anandji Kalyanji Trust of Ahmedabad, which maintains multiple Jain temples in the country, is more than three hundred years old. And in registrars' offices across India, you can come across wills and testaments of devout Muslim ladies going back centuries, who have endowed land and buildings for the benefit of future pilgrims and students.

The *Isavasya Upanishad* makes clear that the Lord pervades the universe and that we hold this earth as trustees of the Lord. Mahatma Gandhi borrowed from English legal traditions, the Gujarati Bania tradition and the *Isavasya Upanishad* to come up with his ideas on trusteeship. In her famous speech in Stockholm, Indira Gandhi quoted from the *Atharva Veda* to affirm that we as humans need to be gentle with Mother Earth as she needs to sustain our children and future generations to come. All of these intellectual sources lead to a solid conservative case for our acting as trustees of our land.

And there is an aesthetic element to it. If tomorrow we were to lose banyan and pipal trees, tigers, kites, blackbucks, elephants, koels and bulbuls, would we have any art remaining? If our rivers dry up, will Vrindavan,

Avantika and Srirangam lose their physicality and turn into museum metaphors? If the Ganga is not restored, will there be an idea of India to contend with? Will we stop reading Pandit Nehru's luminous will, where he makes the case that the Ganga and the idea of India are intertwined.

It is fashionable to criticize maharajas. They did not let their subjects hunt in the jungles, which they kept for themselves. The unintended consequence was that our forests were preserved. The British did a fair amount of damage by viewing forests not as trusts but as commercial logging opportunities, by overindulging in shikar and by introducing German monocultural practices. Luckily, some of them did try to undo this damage, at least to a limited extent. Through the 1950s and 1960s, we did a terrible job with our ecology. We ignored our forests. Luckily for us, Indira Gandhi turned out to be a stern environmentalist. Whatever her other faults, she saved at least some of our forest cover, wetlands and reserves.

Today we have reached an excruciating impasse. There is acute population pressure at the peripheries of all our reserves and even in their core areas. There are increasing demands for highways that cut across forest corridors. Ironically, we have a lot of mineral wealth in our forest regions. This fact is forcing painful choices that we would rather not make.

Balancing these factors is the growth of ecotourism among our middle classes. Environmentalism is no longer confined to maharajas or Indira Gandhi. There are some technocratic solutions on the horizon. If we improve our agricultural practices, we can easily reduce the quantum of cultivated land that we need and we can start returning degraded lands that are adjacent to forests to the denizens of the jungle.

But technocratic solutions alone will not suffice. We need to somehow improve our abilities in the realm of dialogue. We need to be able to sit down and converse with each other about the trade-offs between dams, tribal rights, mining requirements, highways, population pressures, animal corridors and human–animal conflicts.

Unfortunately, the civic space for dialogue has shrunk. Instead, we are faced with shrill and obdurate extremists on all sides. De Tocqueville made the case that town meetings may hold the key to the success of the gradual approach to change so successfully practised in Anglo-Saxon democracies. We need to resort to such exercises rather than the purely adversarial legal processes that we have become habituated to. I believe that Burkean conservatives have a distinct role to play in encouraging this dialogue, in appealing to our ancient traditions of trusteeship, and in emphasizing the shared mutuality of the political sphere. I am grateful to Ram Guha for drawing my attention to the fact that conservatism and conservation are words with the same root. The categorical imperative for conservatives is therefore that much stronger. Because this is going to be difficult does not mean that we can or we should walk away. Let us draw inspiration from the great conservative philosopher Tiruvalluvar, who constantly emphasized the character traits of bravery, resilience and fortitude in the performance of difficult duties.

Conclusion

I spent some time thinking about how one ends a meandering text of this kind, and discussing this with my friends and family. The consensus that emerged is that some broad ideas need to be restated. Despite my conservatism, I am tempted to resort to the regrettable modern habit of summarizing in bullet points:

- The ancient Indian traditions of conservatism start with the Shanti Parva of the Mahabharata and the Tirukkural. The focus is on how human beings tread between the creative tensions implied in the pursuit of the three human goals of artha or economic and political activity, kama or affairs of passion, and dharma or the challenges of virtue and ethical conduct. The fourth human pursuit, moksha or salvation, follows if the first three are properly addressed. Clearly, the unit of our concern is the individual. However, individuals do live in societies and artha, kama and dharma can only be pursued in a social and political context. This context must favour the full flourishing of individuals and requires restraint on the part of a sovereign, who is simultaneously firm when required. The endless cogitations on the principle of Raja Dharma mandate the creation of an atmosphere where the free individual is not intimidated or overpowered by the prevalence of tyranny in the form of Matsya Nyaya, where the big fish eat the small.

- After the purusharthas of artha (economic and political activity), dharma (virtue and ethical conduct), kama (passion and the aesthetic pursuits), the second and possibly most important contribution of ancient India to the doctrines of conservatism is the concept of Yuga Dharma, or mores and practices that evolve in concord with changing times. This concept goes back some 2500 years to the Apastamba Sutra of the *Yajur Veda*. While the pursuit of dharma as virtue retains its importance eternally, the form of dharma must change with the times. Or as Burke would have it, we need to change and reform in order to conserve. A call by virtually every sensitive Indian that caste, for instance, needs to be extensively transformed and perhaps dropped altogether in our age would be a good example of how Yuga Dharma manifests itself.

- The *Atharva Veda* and the *Isavasya Upanishad* anticipate the English common law idea of trusteeship, particularly as it deals with land. We are trustees with a fiduciary responsibility to ensure that the land we inherit from our ancestors is passed on as is or in a better state to our descendants. It is appropriate that we pass on not just the land but the ideas, the culture, the arts, the thoughts, the philosophies that we are fortunate to inherit, again intact or in a better form.

- The two founders of modern Indian conservatism are Rammohun Roy and Bankim Chandra Chatterjee. Rammohun Roy is solidly in the tradition of Burke. He has given us the legacy of the Rammohun Roy trick, which enables us to advocate the abandonment of so-called recently acquired traditions, by reaching back to presumably more hallowed older ones. Bankim can be considered the founder of the Hindu nationalist school of conservatism. The moderate strain in this school can be seen as a subset of Indian conservatism.

- Indian economic conservatives have been defenders of the market, in line with their intellectual affiliation not only to Burke and Adam Smith, but also to the ideals of the Tirukkural and persistent Indian institutions like the mandi and the bazaar. The failure of the Raj to protect free markets was followed by a ferocious assault on the market by the government of free India. This has left Indians poorer and less free than we would have otherwise been. Recent partial corrections are slowly healing these self-imposed ailments. But we must not rest easy. All of India's political groups seem to have an enduring fondness for statism. In the absence of vigilance, this proclivity will keep trying to resurrect itself. Fighting this Raktabeeja, or demon who gets resurrected even as his blood is shed, has to be a central plank of our dharma.

- In the cultural sphere, Indian conservatives are vociferous defenders of an overarching Indian culture imagined in antiquity and evolving over time. We reject the argument that this is a modern upper-caste Hindu reactionary construct. Its Hindu flavour notwithstanding, it transcends religions as well as ethnicities, languages and regions and is informed by the spirit of diversity and paradox implied in the expression 'bahuratna vasundhara', suggesting that the earth of India is studded with many gems.

- In the social sphere, we are witness to some fine examples of Disraeli's prescription of preserving the best from the past while abandoning the worst. We see this in matters like the changing contours of caste, the evolving nature of our religions, the strides that we are making in gender relations – mostly on a voluntary, gradual, organic basis. State intervention has presented both pluses and minuses in this area.

- In the aesthetic sphere, we have much to be proud of. The embrace of the diversities and the vibrancies present in our country has led to an extraordinary modern efflorescence. Only, some areas like education and public architecture have been cramped by the suffocating grip of the state. A certain amount of national homogenization on account of art forms like the cinema, and quasi-religious activities like cricket, is happening, again on a voluntary, gradual, organic basis and this needs to be lauded. Our performance on guarding our environment as trustees in the conservative fashion has been very spotty. Failure to improve in this area could lead to our grandchildren being overwhelmed by the Great Indian Desert.

- In the political sphere, the principal twentieth-century conundrum has been as to how to approach the Raj. Given the deep feelings surrounding foreign imperial rule, it has been difficult to appreciate the positions of so many stalwarts that there was much good in the Raj and its finer legacies need to be preserved. This has been an uphill battle. Leftists have criticized conservatives as being comprador collaborators. Conservatives have also been criticized by elements of the right as being rootless Macaulay-putras. Despite these disputes being loud in college debating societies, Indian ground realities have ignored criticisms from both the left and the right. Our Supreme Court continues to quote the Magna Carta and the English principles of equity; our armed forces refuse to undertake coups; we change governments at the polls and not by firing whiffs of grapeshot. Above all, Indian parents in every corner of the country keep trying their best to send their children to English-medium schools. The real world of the swain or the common people, as Burke would have referred to it, trumps the cant of the ideologues.

- In free India, with the failure of the Swatantra experiment, it has now become clear that a political party in the Burke–Rammohun Roy–Gokhale–Rajagopalachari mode has little chance of success. Luckily, we have the Rajni Kothari trick. This involves influencing political parties from the outside through debate and dialogue, but more importantly through influencing caucuses inside the parties who are sympathetic to different aspects of conservatism.

Conclusion

Now for the summary closing benediction, if you will, even if some of it is repetitive.

Indian conservatives must continue to push for greater reliance on market-friendly solutions. In the absence of this, we will remain a poor country. But there is a moral reason also to support markets – they represent one of the highest and most sophisticated forms of free, civilized human intercourse.

We must stand firm that there is something known as Indian culture and an idea of India, which we define in our vocabulary, ignoring the barbs of derisive foreign academics and their Indian counterparts. We must continue to push for social reform and religious evolution through consensual, legislative, non-violent means where we do not throw out the baby with the bathwater.

In the political sphere, we must advocate both inside political formations through caucuses and from outside through dialogue. We must recognize moderate Hindu nationalism as a legitimate movement inside the conservative tent. It is particularly important insofar as it is more market friendly than other dispensations and can defend our culture against Marxist and Freudian attacks. It is not without its problems as the commitment to free markets is not unambiguous. And if there remains a continued inability or an unwillingness to control extreme elements and extremism, it can never be conservative.

Extremism has an unerring instinct: sooner or later, it devours its children.

In the aesthetic sphere, the time has not come for us to get seriously worried about being smothered by global homogenization or about our audiences losing interest in our rather grand and graceful heritage. If we do not pay attention to our role as trustees of the land that stretches from the Bridge on the Ocean to the Abode of Snow, we run the risk of leaving behind a desert for our grandchildren. We would then have failed in living up to the most important of conservative ideals – the ideal that we are part of a contract both with our ancestors and with our descendants.

~

As I read the preceding paragraphs they appear to me to be almost a quasi-manifesto for Indian conservative action. But if one were to stay true to the conservative spirit, one needs to appeal for the creation of a temperament and an attitude, not a call to action alone. The message of focusing on both temperament and action is what I would like to leave behind as my plea to my readers.

The attitude must be to see our history as a continuum, and in that history to see the trajectory of free India not as being violently disconnected from its immediate past – the Raj. The Raj itself must be viewed as the proverbial curate's egg – both good and bad in parts. Among the Raj's dubious legacies is the patronizing approach to Indian culture.

Unfortunately, the approach of powerful contemporary vested interests is actually infinitely worse than that of the Raj, where redeeming voices were present. The description of a non-existent but apparently malign upper-caste male Hindu tradition – hegemonic, reactionary, oppressive and patriarchal – has gained sanction based on the efforts of sinister Marxist, Freudian and postmodernist practitioners of dubious integrity and bizarre intelligence, if that is the word we wish to use.

Luckily for us, we remain a young, vigorous and energized nation, unlike the decrepit failing states of Europe that seem to have succumbed to shame and guilt over their colonial past, whose churches are empty, whose birth rate is declining perilously, whose family life is falling apart with a growing number of children born out of wedlock, whose population is old and tired, and that have lost the will to defend the legacy of their ancestors. Their joys are largely superficial and hedonistic.

We are far from that place. But we need to be eternally vigilant. A sober temperament and a balanced attitude can always be made to look unfashionable when confronted with hysterical grievance-mongering.

The Raj helped us get acquainted with Burke and Adam Smith. Luckily for us, as we delve into our own past, we can fall back on the Shanti Parva of the Mahabharata, on Tiruvalluvar, on the Apastamba Sutra, on the *Atharva Veda*, on so much more. It is to our individual and national character or charitra that we need to remain faithful. That will provide the temperament and attitude that our ancestors have given us as their gift, and which we need to pass on to our descendants. Action, while important, is almost secondary. It is to the preservation of our intellectual legacy, a legacy that is touched by the sacred, that we need to stay committed, and to turn to its timeless wisdom for guidance, both as individuals and as a nation.

Guide for Further Reading

Given the discursive, anecdotal, conversational and elliptic structure of my book, my editor and I both felt that a footnoted quasi-academic book is not something we should aim for. But the book is full of references and casual citations. It was simply inappropriate to leave the 'references' part unaddressed. So here is an attempt. The principal aim of this section is not to prove or cite with academic rigour, but to encourage readers to explore further reading at their own pace, partly in order to better understand the philosophy of conservatism and the impressive nature of Indian conservatism and to deal with their own personal concerns and intellectual conundrums. So what follows is the very antithesis of a page-wise, line-wise bibliography.

I am assuming that most of my readers will access the Shanti Parva of the Mahabharata (Sanskrit original), the Apastamba Sutra (Sanskrit original), the *Atharva Veda* (Sanskrit original), Tiruvalluvar's

Tirukkural (Tamil original) and Allasami Peddanna's 'Manucharitamu' (Telugu original) in translations. It is always best to start with a conservative editor and translator. C. Rajagopalachari's prose versions of the Mahabharata and the Tirukkural are the best places to begin.

In recent times, Bibek Debroy has come out with a magnificent and awesome ten-volume rendition of the Mahabharata. Readers would do well to buy all ten volumes, now available in a box set. Volume eight is the Shanti Parva – and what a grand book it is! I would also advise my readers not to waste their time with the internet-driven controversies about what has been inserted later and what is original. These are typical orientalist analytical obsessions. The Magna Carta is admired not because it was written by venal and selfish barons – it is admired for its spirit. So too with the Shanti Parva. The discussions on Raja Dharma are a unique and important contribution to our collective human legacy in the realm of political philosophy. And if you are really interested in the eternal problem of the intersection between individual dharma and collective dharma, do read Gurcharan Das's *The Difficulty of Being Good*. There is no better text on the perennial and never-ending obsession that Indians have with this overworked word, dharma.

As to the Prithvi Sukta of the *Atharva Veda*, I could recommend many translations but, to be honest, I think the reader would do well to simply explore the Web – there are enough interesting and brilliant versions floating around.

As far as the Apastamba Sutra of the *Yajur Veda* is concerned, I would like to let the reader enter a personal secret cavern of mine. I may be lapsed, but my ancestors were and have been Yajurvedi Brahmins (pretty low in the hierarchy as they were primarily performing duties like cleaning, fixing, arranging – they were not chanting and, the Gods forbid, they were not conducting sacrifice rituals). And guess what – my ancestors belonged to the Apastamba Sutra, not the more aristocratic Baudhayana Sutra. In any event, it is the Apastamba Sutra that talks about Yuga Dharma. The great P.V. Kane's seminal book on the subject, *A History of the Dharmashastra*, is probably out of print, so for those interested a used book website would be the best place to go.

As far as the Tirukkural is concerned, for readers who like a Victorian/stentorian style, I believe Reverend G.U. Pope's translation has been republished by AES. Otherwise, just buy C. Rajagopalachari's version available in a nice Bharatiya Vidya Bhavan paperback; or if you have the time and inclination for a little more intellectual challenge, P.S. Sundaram's paperback is a favourite of mine. It is important to keep in mind that the 'this-wordly' Tiruvalluvar is always and continually interested in the 'correct' way to live as individuals, as productive citizens, as farmers, as wealthy persons, as kings, and even as writers!

We are lucky that in the Murty Classical Library series, the illustrious Israeli Indologist David Shulman has published a translation of Peddanna's Telugu classic 'Manucharitamu'.

For readers in search of moral instruction, I would advise skipping the *Markandeya Purana* and going straight to Jaishankar Prasad's modern Hindi epic poem 'Kamayani' with its metaphorical characters, now available in English translation.

C. Rajagopalachari goes beyond the Mahabharata and the Tirukkural. He is the Bhishma of Indian conservatism. His chaste and lucid writings in the *Swarajya* are now being reprinted in the revived *Swarajya*, and are always worth reading. Rajmohan Gandhi's biography of Rajagopalachari has to be one of the most lucid, balanced and empathetic biographies that have been written.

Modern conservatism starts with Edmund Burke. So it is to Burke that I must direct my readers with some emphasis. I would strongly recommend that before plunging into Burke's works, they get acquainted with Burke's life through a brilliant book: *The Great Melody* by Conor Cruise O'Brien. My friend and boss Kantic Dasgupta lent me this book many years ago. My continuing admiration for Burke is grounded in this book. Burke should be savoured in small doses. *A Vindication of Natural Societies* and *A Philosophical Enquiry into the Origins of Our Ideas of the Sublime and Beautiful* are traditionally assigned the positions of authentic original Burkean classics. It must be remembered that these are early works. The evolution of his ideas and his emergence as a full-blown philosopher of what can only be called practical and beautiful traditions reach a kind of apogee in *On American Taxation* and *Reflections on the Revolution in France*. Indian readers would do well to access Burke's parliamentary speeches, including of course his magisterial 'Impeachment of Warren Hastings'. My father was particularly fond of Burke's speech in the House of Commons on the Nawab of Arcot's debts. A more brilliant conservative indictment of rapacious imperialism has rarely been presented. Contemporary readers who are into water conservation may note Burke's praise for India's traditional kings who built canals and reservoirs and fulfilled their obligations to unborn generations of the future! O'Brien makes the case that Burke opposed George III and Pitt apropos of Indian administration. If Burke's proposals for oversight of the East India Company Government by Parliamentary Commissioners instead of the Crown had prevailed, the Indo-British connection may have been more supple, more productive and perhaps even more enduring. As an aside, Macaulay's tidy little essay on the Hastings Impeachment as a spectacle makes for interesting diversionary reading.

Moving on to Adam Smith and David Hume, I would recommend a similar approach. I would start with the brilliant biographies of these Scotsmen by Nicholas Phillipson. These are now available in relatively slim paperbacks. The Adam Smith biography was particularly useful for me because Phillipson quotes extensively from Burke's review of Smith's *Theory of Moral Sentiments*, where Burke makes specific reference to my favourite 'wisdom of the swain'. Phillipson also analyses at some length Smith's position on India and his dislike of the East India Company. All of us are required to say that we have read Smith's *An Inquiry into the Nature and Causes of the Wealth of Nations* even if only to be able to pretend that we are authentically quoting its most famous line. I would submit that this classic is worth reading for more than just one sentence. Most people miss Smith's *Theory of Moral Sentiments*, and that is a mistake. I was very fortunate that no less a person than Amartya Sen directed me to this magnificent work. This work is central to the evolution of the moral philosophy of conservatism – and what is conservatism if not a moral philosophy. Hume's *An Enquiry Concerning Human Understanding* is important in order to understand how conservatism and empiricism are inextricably tied up.

Hobbes had his *Leviathan* and Locke had *An Essay Concerning Human Understanding*. Both are important reference works for any serious reader. It is important to remember that these were all thinkers writing at a time when clear-cut labels like conservatism and liberalism with all their limiting portents were yet to take birth.

The Federalist Papers written by the American freedom fighters Madison, Hamilton and Jay are actually quite easy to read and I would strongly recommend them to my readers. They are foundational documents for conservatism as it emerged on the western side of the Atlantic. As I have argued, the American Declaration of Independence and the opening parts of the US Constitution, while the products of a 'revolution', were and remain evolutionary conservative documents. They are worth reading again and again. It is important to remember that Ambedkar and his colleagues in our Constituent Assembly drew inspiration from them.

Alexis de Tocqueville's *Democracy in America* is an absolute must-read. It is only after reading de Tocqueville that I began to appreciate clubs (very English, and now not that uncommon in India) and sangeet sabhas (very Indian, in fact probably very south Indian!). The importance of voluntary civic associations outside the purview of the state and the sovereign in the sustenance of communities and the larger nation cannot be overemphasized. This is why totalitarians hate them. It is to de Tocqueville's credit that he understood the importance of these voluntary community associations long ago.

Disraeli was not just a politician. He was a novelist of some distinction. I consider his novel *Coningsby* to be one of the best treatises on conservatism. Henry Maine's *Ancient Law* was a prize book that my grandfather had won in college. I used to see it in his shelves and got to read it much after my grandfather's death. It is dated and certainly subject to much revisionism. But the fact remains that Maine did look for the organic nature of the evolution of human legal systems – a subject of great interest to conservatives. Maine lived in India and his *Village-Communities in the East and West*, which again though dated and probably based on inadequate research, is important because his idealized Indian village became part of the grammar of Gandhian thought and was opposed by Nehru, Ambedkar and others. It is only in recent times that many have escaped the clutches of Maine's thoughts and tried to view urban, mercantile, trading and even pilgrim-bound India as more central than the India of isolated autarkic villages.

F.W. Maitland's *The Constitutional History of England* is a magisterial work and is an absolute must for anyone interested in understanding the deep Anglo-Saxon roots of conservatism. Of course, I am hoping that my readers will see parallels and synchronicity with Indian texts. Alan Macfarlane's *The Making of the Modern World: Visions from the West and East* does an outstanding job of comparing two great conservatives – Maitland from England and Yukichi Fukuzawa from Japan.

Roger Scruton is perhaps the greatest living English conservative philosopher. His recent popular books, *How to Be a Conservative* and *Conservatism: An Invitation to the Great Tradition*, are simple, lucid and incandescent – must-reads even if you don't want to be a conservative. For the more adventurous, his three books – *Conservative Thoughts*, *Conservative Thinkers* and *Conservative Texts* – are pure and simple gold mines. For those who love polemics, his

Thinkers of the New Left is a comprehensive demolition of the pretensions of Marxist and postmodern absurdities. Virtually everything that Scruton has written or still writes is worth reading. But if the reader has to draw the line, there it rests.

Benedict Anderson's figure and presence are recurring motifs for all students of modern political movements. While his *Imagined Communities* may be viewed as obligatory reading, many of his other writings too are of considerable interest and significance.

Rammohun Roy said and did so many things in such a variegated life that we don't know where to begin. But my view is that we should be very careful about evaluating Rammohun – I wrote a poem once that included a couple of lines about the fact that Rammohun was buried 'outside' holy India. The fact is that Rammohun belonged to the world, not just to us. H.D. Sharma and Bruce Robertson have written the most useful books on him. So while the reader is welcome to try and access Rammohun Roy in the original, I would strongly suggest Sharma and Robertson as good introductions.

Bankim must not be read through interlocutors or biographers who quote from him. He was a creative writer and in many respects 'the father of the Indian historical novel'. *Anandamath* is available in popular paperbacks and it is a must-read to understand the complex/complicated/difficult Hindu response to British rule. Bankim captured the essence of what my own ancestors felt in distant Coimbatore – that British rule was a liberating and empowering phenomenon. *Anandamath* is not optional – it is required reading for the serious or even semi-serious reader. As far as *Durgeshnandini* and Bankim's other works are concerned, I would say they are optional but recommended!

Dadhabhai Naoroji's *Poverty and Un-British Rule in India* is a classic. It needs to be read if for no other reason than the fact that Naoroji is able to exercise sobriety even when dealing with the hypersensitive topic of an organized system of plundering the surpluses of a subject country.

Romesh Chandra Dutt's two volumes on *The Economic History of India* are not to be missed. The serious lapses in Raja Dharma on the part of our British rulers come through in an incandescent manner. Conservatives should note that Dutt was also an early and brilliant translator of the Mahabharata!

'Shenoy: The Forgotten Economist' is a good essay in *Swarajya* which, among other things, captures the tragedy of our country that chose not to listen to honest Cassandras. B.R. Shenoy's 'Note of Dissent', submitted during the formulation of the Second Five Year Plan, is one of those awesome documents that can be seen as an appeal to the brooding spirit of common sense in history. The Centre for Civil Society has put out an excellent pamphlet on Shenoy.

Jean Drèze and Amartya Sen's *An Uncertain Glory: India and Its Contradictions* captures the story of the poor and misplaced capacity of the contemporary Indian state. Deepak Lal's *The Hindu Equilibrium* and *In Praise of Empires* cover economic and political history with rare panache.

Jadunath Sarkar's histories of the Mughals, Aurangzeb and Shivaji are gems not only of deep historical scholarship but of stately English prose. Dipesh Chakravarti's recent book on Sarkar captures the latter's central interest in 'character' as a determinant of history. It is important to read K.M. Munshi, especially his fictional works like *Jaya Somnath*, in order to understand a significant trend in Hindu nationalism that emanates from outside the Bengal–Punjab–Maharashtra tripod.

Nilakanta Sastri's *A History of South India* remains an evergreen work, despite the numerous and even successful revisionist approaches that have attempted to replace his vision. The bird's-eye view retains its charms.

R.C. Majumdar edited the eleven-volume magnum opus on Indian history produced by the Bharatiya Vidya Bhavan. It remains a foundational work of historical conservatism. Its Hindu flavour is not an accident – it is a well thought-out intellectual exercise.

D.B. Parasnis's *A History of the Maratha People* and G.S. Sardesai's *A History of Modern India in Three Parts* brightened the Maratha historical horizon in different ways. Their neglect in recent times is sad indeed. I do recommend readers to search out their works.

Two writers on Maratha history who are not referred to

in my book may be central to understanding conservatism in western India. They have certainly influenced me. The first is the Scotsman Dennis Kincaid, who learnt Marathi and who captures the full flavour of what he saw as the brilliant Maratha interregnum between the Mughals and the British. The second is Manohar Malgonkar, whose works on Kanhoji Angre, Nana Sahib and the Puars of Dewas are currently neglected at great cost to our collective intellectual development. It should not go unmentioned that Malgonkar was a leading light of the Swatantra Party!

I have made references to the histories of India by A.L. Basham and Percival Spear. It is important to note that not all foreign scholars can be dismissed as orientalists. These two possess a rare integrity and a felicity that deserves the attention of more readers. (I especially recommend Basham's *The Wonder That Was India* and Spear's *A History of India*, Volume 2). The two volumes of Nirad Chaudhuri's autobiography are very helpful for anyone trying to take a journey through modern Indian history. His *Continent of Circe* and *Hinduism: A Religion to Live By* are cheeky, irreverent and frequently wrong. But the innate restrained satire of the classic conservative is never absent.

Three histories that cannot be ignored are V.P. Menon's *Transfer of Power in India*, Durga Das's *From Curzon to Nehru and After* and Narendra Singh Sarila's *The Shadow of the Great Game*. Zareer Masani's work on Macaulay and Meghnad Desai's *The Rediscovery of India* are important correctives for the usual anti-Raj bombast that emanates from the NCERT.

Ramachandra Guha's comprehensive *India After Gandhi* should by all accounts become a prescribed text. I have received feedback that I have been a bit unfair in alleging Soviet and crypto-Marxist influence at the highest levels of independent India's government. The diaries of the former KGB agent Mitrokhin amply demonstrate that, if anything, I might have understated the Soviet impact.

Surendranath Dasgupta's *History of Indian Philosophy*, M. Hiriyanna's *Essentials of Indian Philosophy* and S. Radhakrishnan's *The Hindu View of Life* are all available in numerous current editions. Their importance is in re-establishing the respectability of Indian philosophy in our own eyes, let alone in the eyes of our British rulers.

G.S. Ghurye is neglected as he is not 'fashionable' in Marxist and postmodern terms. But not reading *The Scheduled Tribes of India* would be a serious mistake for anyone who wants to understand the issues before us as a people. Verrier Elwin is always a difficult read and his books tend to be out of print. Ramachandra Guha's biography of Elwin, *Savaging the Civilized*, gives a good overall coverage to alternate views on the tribals of India.

Ananda Coomaraswamy's *The Dance of Shiva* is a must. His other works, all quite illuminating, can be considered optional.

Gopal Krishna Gokhale is best approached through his

biographies by Govind Talwalkar and B.R. Nanda. The latter is somewhat out of fashion now. But when I read him first, it made a solid impression on me, which remains unchanged. Stanley Wolpert's *Tilak and Gokhale* is useful because he manages to juxtapose Gokhale's Burkean position with the rather more radical Hindu view that is associated with Tilak.

Jawaharlal Nehru's *The Discovery of India* and his 'Last Will and Testament' represent high-water marks of English prose and a sensitive Indian persona. He never called himself a conservative. But his writings do show that at times he had the proper (!) conservative predilections.

An excellent anthology of B.R. Ambedkar's writings has been put together by Christophe Jaffrelot and Narendra Kumar. Ambedkar's evidence before the Southborough Committee and the Simon Commission are printed in full. These brilliant tracts are a prelude to his December 1946 speech to the Constituent Assembly where there is an extensive quotation from who else but Edmund Burke. Just warms the hearts of conservatives! Sitting in the same Constituent Assembly was the young Minoo Masani, whose various works, particularly *Against the Tide,* represent a lament for the years India lost to dirigiste socialism.

Swapan Dasgupta's *Awakening Bharat Mata* is an extremely timely and useful book. Here, in a single volume, one gets to read the views of diverse voices within the Hindu nationalist world view. It is to Dasgupta's credit that he has included in its entirety Bhandarkar's 1895 speech, which in my opinion represents the high-water mark of nineteenth-century Indian conservatism. Vikram Sampath's and Vaibhav Purandare's recent biographies of Savarkar and the authoritative studies on the RSS by Walter Andersen and Shridhar Damle are of great importance in understanding Hindu nationalism in a balanced manner. Too many other works start with a leftist prejudice that is more interested in self-centred navel-gazing and sanctimonious verbiage than in understanding the subject. Tathagata Roy's biography of Shyamaprasad Mukherjee is the best source on his life. It is a comprehensive and sympathetic account.

It is an ancient Indian tradition in philosophical debates to summarize the views of one's opponents. It is only with this in mind that I recommend reading Wendy Doniger's tiring and tiresome works on Hinduism. A good contrast is to be found in the works of Diana Eck. Diana Eck is in the good company of Heinrich Zimmer with his *Myths and Symbols in Indian Art and Civilization* and Richard Blurton with his *The Art of Hindu India*.

Sir Syed Ahmad Khan was a formidable scholar. If possible, readers should try to access his *Causes of the Indian Revolt*. It is difficult to understand the Raj's impact on our country without taking Sir Syed's views into account. Whatever one's views on him, Iqbal's *Complaint to God*, available in different translations, is required reading in order to understand the separatist, exclusivist political movement that developed in the first half of the twentieth century. His speeches tend to be repetitive but are not without substance. His poem on Cordoba demonstrates a little understood strain of pan-Islamism. Rafiq Zakaria's biography of Iqbal praises the subject somewhat effusively; nevertheless it is useful reading.

Ashis Nandy's *The Intimate Enemy* is an absolute must for anyone trying to put together an understanding of this complex, aggravating and puzzling peninsula in our times. His *Tao of Cricket* is going to be seen as a classic in the years to come.

Sudhir Kakar's *Inner World* is important for all of us caught up in the confusions and conundrums of modern India.

I have frequently referred to Maasti Venkatesh Iyengar, the great Kannada writer. His *Chikkaveera Rajendra* is available in English translation. There is also a gem of a movie made around his drama *Kaakana Kotey*.

More than his *Midnight's Children*, Salman Rushdie's *The Moor's Last Sigh* captures the canvas of modern Indian culture with superb aplomb.

And, of course, we cannot even begin to try and understand modern India without paying attention to V.S. Naipaul. His Indian trilogy (*An Area of Darkness*, *A Wounded Civilization* and *A Million Mutinies Now*) can be hurtful at times. But the three books are never without insights. Swapan Dasgupta in his recent book has reprinted the complete text of Naipaul's interview with Dileep Padgaonkar. Well worth a read.

Acknowledgements

My friend Kamal Sharma, the inveterate Anglophile Dogra has been responsible for making sure that I never deviated from the path of conservatism.

My friend and boss Kantic Dasgupta, who let me borrow O'Brien's biography of Edmund Burke, thus introducing me to a special world.

My friend Seetharam, who has all along maintained that the conservative writings in classical Tamil represent some of humanity's best moments.

My friends Ravi Bahl and Samit Ghosh, for tolerating my conservative 'excesses' and sometimes egging me on.

My friend Rajesh Singh, for himself epitomizing conservatism in more ways than one.

My friend Shekhar Gupta, for allowing and encouraging me to inflict my conservatism on the readers of the *Indian Express*.

Acknowledgements

My friend Saubhik Chakravarti, for prodding me on ceaselessly and for coming up with the title of my earlier book, *Notes from an Indian Conservative*.

My friend R. Vaidyanathan, for refusing to modify or sugarcoat his position as a Hindu conservative in his conversations with me.

My friend Dilip George Kuruvilla (George K.), who effortlessly articulated the enduring Indian tryst with androgyny.

My friend Anmol Vellani, for forcing me to stop ducking away from the dangers of a convenient consequentialism.

My friend the healer par excellence Dr Farokh Udwadia, who seeks to conserve the conservative spirit of T.S. Eliot.

My friends Prasanna Viswanathan, Amar Govindarajan, Sandipan Deb and R. Jagannathan for my *Swarajya* connect.

My American friend Rick Braddock, who epitomizes for me the American conservative spirit.

This book itself germinated from a series of lectures I gave at Ashoka University, thanks to an invitation from Rudrangshu Mukherjee and support from Venkat Eshwara. Rudrangshu gave me important feedback on my text. My son Vijay went through the first draft with a fine-tooth comb and came up with numerous insights and suggestions. His intimate knowledge of American conservatism was of great help to me. His keen ear helped detect avoidable transgressions of good prose style. My friend the historian Ram Guha very kindly spent a lot of time giving me tons of inputs, correcting some of my factual errors and sparring with me on various matters. In some sense, Ram's lament a few years ago about the need for a conservative intellectual discourse in contemporary India has been doing the rounds among many of us, who have felt the need to respond to his challenge. Swaminathan Aiyar challenged me considerably and forced me to go back and relook at modern Indian history. The affable Kiran Karnik took time to read my draft and help me flesh out some ideas. The ever supportive, gentle and erudite Gurcharan Das was particularly helpful in getting me to think about providing readers with an appropriate list for further reading. Dipesh Chakravarti and Swapan Dasgupta, in irrepressible probashi style, forced me to think of 'character' as being central to conservative thought. The dynamic publisher of Juggernaut, Chiki Sarkar, was a joy to deal with. My editor at Juggernaut, Nandini Mehta, was just terrific. Nandini's colleague Cincy Jose has dealt with my tantrums with patience and sensitivity. My agent, Kanishka Gupta, was a special friend during some dark times. My family – my wife, Neelambari, and my three children, Vijay, Sanju and Raghav, were forced to have this book read to them on numerous occasions, chapter by tiresome chapter, while being inundated with emails containing long word files. But they did not give up on me.

The errors, the exaggerations, the stylistic problems and so many other negatives in the book are all mine.

THE APP FOR INDIAN READERS

Fresh, original books tailored for mobile and for India. Starting at ₹10.

juggernaut.in

1

CRAFTED FOR MOBILE READING

Thought you would never read a book on mobile? Let us prove you wrong.

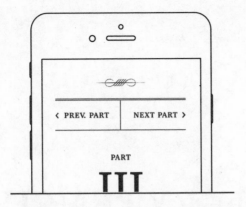

Beautiful Typography

The quality of print transferred
to your mobile. Forget ugly PDFs.

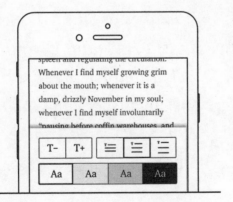

Customizable Reading

Read in the font size, spacing
and background of your liking.

AN EXTENSIVE LIBRARY

Including fresh, new, original Juggernaut books from the likes of Sunny Leone, Praveen Swami, Husain Haqqani, Umera Ahmed, Rujuta Diwekar and lots more. Plus, books from partner publishers and loads of free classics. Whichever genre you like, there's a book waiting for you.

3

❋

DON'T
JUST READ;
INTERACT

We're changing the reading experience from passive to active.

juggernaut.in

Ask authors questions

Get all your answers from the horse's mouth.
Juggernaut authors actually reply to every
question they can.

Rate and review

Let everyone know of your favourite reads or
critique the finer points of a book – you will be
heard in a community of like-minded readers.

Gift books to friends

For a book-lover, there's no nicer gift than
a book personally picked. You can even
do it anonymously if you like.

Enjoy new book formats

Discover serials released in parts over
time, picture books including comics,
and story-bundles at discounted rates.
And coming soon, audiobooks.

4

LOWEST PRICES & ONE-TAP BUYING

Books start at ₹10 with regular discounts and free previews.

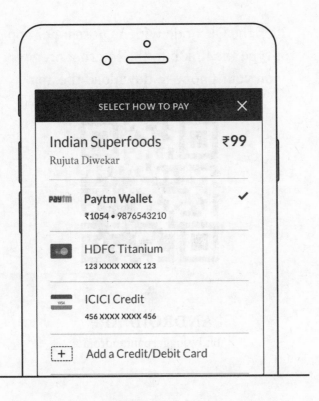

Paytm Wallet, Cards & Apple Payments

On Android, just add a Paytm Wallet once and buy any book with one tap. On iOS, pay with one tap with your iTunes-linked debit/credit card.

Click the QR Code with a QR scanner app
or type the link into the Internet browser
on your phone to download the app.

ANDROID APP
bit.ly/juggernautandroid

iOS APP
bit.ly/juggernautios

For our complete catalogue, visit www.juggernaut.in
To submit your book, send a synopsis and two
sample chapters to books@juggernaut.in
For all other queries, write to contact@juggernaut.in